Building LDAP-Enabled Applications
WITH MICROSOFT®'S ACTIVE DIRECTORY
AND NOVELL®'S NDS

ISBN 0-13-062145-5

90000

9 790130 621459

Building LDAP-Enabled Applications

Applications

WITH MICROSOFT'S ACTIVE DIRECTORY AND NOVELL'S NDS

Bruce Greenblatt

Prentice Hall PTR, Upper Saddle River, NJ 07458
www.phptr.com

Library of Congress Cataloging-in-Publication Data

A CIP catalog record for this book can be obtained from the Library of Congress.

Editorial Production/Composition: *G&S Typesetters, Inc.*
Acquisitions Editor: *Mary Franz*
Editorial Assistant: *Noreen Regina*
Cover Design: *Anthony Gemmellaro*
Cover Director: *Jerry Votta*
Marketing Manager: *Dan DePasquale*
Marketing Manager: *Maura Zaldivar*
Project Coordinator: *Anne R. Garcia*

© 2002 by Prentice Hall PTR
Prentice-Hall, Inc.
Upper Saddle River, New Jersey 07458

Prentice Hall books are widely used by corporations and government agencies for training, marketing, and resale.
The publisher offers discounts on this book when ordered in bulk quantities. For more information, contact:

Corporate Sales Department
Prentice Hall PTR
One Lake Street
Upper Saddle River, NJ 07458
Phone: 800-382-3419; FAX: 201-236-7141
E-mail (Internet): corpsales@prenhall.com

Printed in the United States of America

10   9   8   7   6   5   4   3   2   1

ISBN 0-13-062145-5

Pearson Education Ltd.
Pearson Education Australia PTY, Ltd.
Pearson Education Singapore, Pte. Ltd.
Pearson Education North Asia Ltd.
Pearson Education Canada, Ltd.
Pearson Educación de Mexico, S.A. de C.V.
Pearson Education—Japan
Pearson Education Malaysia, Pte. Ltd.

CONTENTS

ACKNOWLEDGMENTS

From 1998 until mid-2001, I consulted with various companies to help them design and develop LDAP-enabled applications. I'd like to thank the many people that gave me the opportunity to learn more about their applications, and at the same time help them understand how LDAP can be used in various ways in the applications. Mary Franz at Prentice Hall took on the project and helped guide the book. Joshua Goodman and G&S Typesetters gave a level of consistency to the formatting of the book and figures.

The book would not have been nearly as accurate in the technical sense without the contributions of the reviewers, Chris Harding and Alexis Bor. I also thank the many contributors to the standardization efforts of Internet Directories that I've met through the mailing lists and meetings of the Internet Engineering Task Force (IETF). The consistent pressure that is applied to implement and use directories has brought Internet Directories to the state that they are in today.

I would especially like to dedicate this book to my wife Cynthia, without whose love and support I would have never been able to finish the book.

PART ONE

Introduction

CHAPTER OBJECTIVES

Many years ago (in 1983), I was taking a Computer Architecture course in graduate school. Most of the final grade in the course was derived from the semester-long project to design a computer. This project was to be done in three separate parts. Interestingly enough, when we were given the first part of the assignment, we didn't yet know exactly what the second or third parts of the assignment were. The first part of the assignment was to design the "exoarchitecture" of our computer, most of which involved creating the computer's assembly language. Once we had completed that stage, we were handed the second phase of the assignment, which was to design the "endoarchitecture" of our computer. This mostly involved designing the machine language of the computer. In addition, there were specific requirements added to part two that were not mentioned in part one. This was no big deal, except that part two built on part one and we were not allowed to change anything in the design of our exoarchitecture. As might be expected, quite a few students made many mistakes in their designs, which unfortunately had to be carried forward into the later stages of the project. So, of the original 75 or so students, about a third dropped the class after the first phase of the project.

For my part, I had made a choice in phase one to build an 8-bit computer so that the design of the assembly language and its implementation would be simpler. Unfortunately, there were several requirements in phase two that made this a seriously bad choice. Had I known of these requirements, I would have decided to build a 16-bit computer in phase one. This situation is unfortunately common in software development. Midway through the development of a project, new requirements come in and oftentimes seriously invalidate earlier assumptions. If the developers are lucky, they have time to go back and redesign the software system. The students in this class were not so lucky.

The third phase of the project completed the design of the computer. This part of the assignment involved designing much of the "microarchitecture" of the computer, which revolves around the microprogramming aspects of the hardware. Again, this assignment included some new requirements that made some of the students' earlier choices unfortunate. So, at the end of the three phases of the course project, I had assembled a seriously convoluted design for a computer. Many students had similar stories, and other students weren't around to complete the project. Only 22 of the original 75 students remained to the bitter end. Of these, only 11 received a passing grade (I was fortunate enough to be among that number).

While there were many books available that described existing computer architectures (most of them used the IBM 360 series mainframe as the principle example), very little material described the design process as a whole. Thus, unless we could have had access to Fred Brooks's[1] diaries, we didn't really know what lay ahead of us. Even though the project was an interesting learning experience, it was very difficult to implement a top-notch computer design for this project. In many respects this is similar to the state of affairs of Lightweight Directory Access Protocol (LDAP) integrated application development today. There are several references available that define the basics of LDAP, but nothing is available that goes into any detail of design concepts that are unique to LDAP integrated application development. This book is intended to build on other references that explain the LDAP protocol and the functions of the LDAP Application Programming Interface (API).

What Is Driving LDAP Application Development?

LDAP has been available for several years as an add-on component to various server operating systems. Starting with Windows 2000 Server and NetWare 5.0, the LDAP server is built into the operating system. Windows 2000 Server includes the Active Directory. NetWare 5.0 includes the Novell Directory Service (NDS). So, application developers now have available a new piece of infrastructure technology which will always be available in the most popular network

---

1. Frederick P. Brooks was one of the original designers for the IBM 360 Series. Many of his ideas on the design process are in his classic book *The Mythical Man-Month,* 2d ed. (Boston: Addison-Wesley, 1996).

operating systems. Thus, there is no additional dependency for LDAP-enabled applications that are expected to run on a network, since virtually all local area networks in the future will use either Windows 2000 Server or NetWare 5.0.

The future utilization of LDAP in Internet applications is potentially—if not inevitably—explosive. The corporate networks built using Windows 2000 and NetWare 5.0 are now running the same Transport Control Protocol/Internet Protocol (TCP/IP) based networking protocols that are used on the Internet. This was not true in previous versions of these network operating systems. In the corporate network, LDAP Directories are responsible for making available information about network accessible resources, such as host machines, printers, users, and so forth.

An LDAP Directory provides a set of names and properties in such a way that Directory users can easily search them. Each name in the Directory and its associated properties are collected together as a Directory entry. LDAP Directories operate in client-server mode; LDAP clients submit service requests to Directory servers and Directory servers handle the requests and provide responses to the Directory clients. The core services provided by an LDAP server include property- or attribute-based information storage, manipulation, and retrieval. The most frequently utilized and hence most essential Directory service is *property- or attribute-based information retrieval.* Other services provided by a Directory server, such as data addition, deletion, and modification services, exist to support this primary service and are considered ancillary to the information retrieval service.

Who Is the Target Audience of This Book?

Throughout this book, the explanations of the various components of LDAP technology have been supplemented by making extensive use of examples. The examples of code are written exclusively using the Java programming language. Software developers desiring to create an application that is to be integrated with an LDAP Directory will find the treatment of technology, as well as the data organization in the examples, helpful in their efforts. I believe this to be the case even for developers whose principal programming language is not Java. Thus, the principal target audience for the book includes any application developer that wants to integrate his (or her) application with the network.

What Background Is Needed to Understand This Book?

This book assumes the reader has a basic background in computer science. Nearly all computer professionals will find most of this book easy to understand. Computer programming experience will be very helpful in understanding Chapter 8, Building LDAP Programs Using Java, and Chapter 9, Example LDAP

Applications. The reader does not need to have a deep understanding of computer networking. It is helpful to have experience in using Internet applications, such as a Web Browser.

This book provides basic tutorial information on several different Internet technologies, as well as LDAP itself. Background material in computer networking and security is provided at appropriate points, when this material is needed to provide a complete treatment of the LDAP technology being discussed. This background material is provided for readers with limited backgrounds in those areas.

How to Obtain Documentation on the Internet

LDAP is a specification of the Internet Engineering Task Force (IETF) and provides the specifications that define the protocols that are used in the Internet. The IETF notes on its Web site (located at *www.ietf.org*), "The IETF is a large open international community of network designers, operators, vendors, and researchers concerned with the evolution of the Internet architecture and the smooth operation of the Internet." The IETF publishes its specifications in documents that are known as Requests for Comments (RFCs). RFCs document various aspects of computer communications mainly in the area of protocols that are to be used for the exchange of information between two (or more) Internet hosts. These protocols fall into three main categories:

- Network Layer
- Transport Layer
- Application Layer

An example of a Network Layer protocol is Internet Protocol (IP). Examples of Transport Layer protocols are Transport Control Protocol (TCP) and User Datagram Protocol (UDP). These layers will be summarized in the next chapter. Examples of Application Layer protocols are LDAP and SMTP.

RFCs are freely available from a number of sites around the world, including the IETF's own Web site mentioned above. The work of the IETF that has yet to be published as RFCs is available from these same sites in the form of Internet Drafts. Drafts are work-in-progress documents that are either being investigated by one of the many working groups of the IETF or are individual contributions.

An important difference between IETF and other standards-making bodies in terms of Internet documentation is that IETF documents are always free and, with only very rare exceptions, contain no patented or copyrighted information or ideas. Documentation from virtually every other standards body (e.g., ITU, ANSI, IEEE, ECMA) is prohibitively expensive to obtain. The IETF views this expense as a barrier to the implementation of standards and encourages implementations far and wide. As evidence of this strategy, RFC 2026 (the *Internet Standards Process*) defines the various types of RFCs and the stages in which they proceed. It defines the conditions that must exist before an RFC can proceed from the first level (Proposed Standard) to the first level on the IETF standards track (Draft Standard type RFC). "A specification from which at least two independent and interoperable implementations from different code bases have been developed, and for which sufficient successful operational experience has been obtained, may be elevated to the *Draft Standard* level." Other standard bodies typically introduce their standards prior to any implementation experience.

Organization of This Book

This book contains eleven chapters organized into three parts, arranged as follows:

1. Part I serves as the book's introductory portion. It also provides detailed definitions of the LDAP components that make up the overall service provided by LDAP Directories and the protocols that they use. Chapter 1 sets out the purpose, target audience, and required background for the book. Chapter 2 gives an overview of the Internet and LDAP's place in the Internet. Chapter 3 discusses the Lightweight Directory Access Protocol (LDAP) itself. Chapter 4 discusses LDAP Schema Design. Chapter 5 discusses the various security concepts that are important to LDAP developers.

2. Part II provides an overview of the two principal implementations of LDAP. Chapter 6 gives an overview of how to use an implementation of Active Directory. Chapter 7 provides an overview of how to use an implementation of NDS.

3. Finally, Part III discusses applications of Internet Directories. Chapter 8 provides a quick overview of LDAP and Java. Chapter 9 gives detailed examples of three real-world LDAP-enabled applications. Chapter 10 discusses several limitations of LDAP and how the developer can work around them in the application. Chapter 11 discusses the emerging technology of XML and how it is used in LDAP.

An Overview of LDAP and the Internet

CHAPTER OBJECTIVES

The Internet

Now that the basic concepts of Directories have been introduced, the concepts of the Internet that are important to Directories can be discussed. The term *Internet* refers specifically to the original network that was funded by the United States Department of Defense Advanced Research Projects Agency (ARPA) known as ARPANET. Since its inception in the late 1960s, the ARPANET has evolved into a network that connects millions of hosts across the world. The TCP/IP suite of protocols connects all these hosts. When an Internet-like network is contained inside an enterprise, it has also been called an intranet.

This section will not attempt to explain the entire Internet suite or protocol stack. It will take the perspective of viewing the Internet stack from the perspective of a Directory and will discuss which parts of the Internet suite

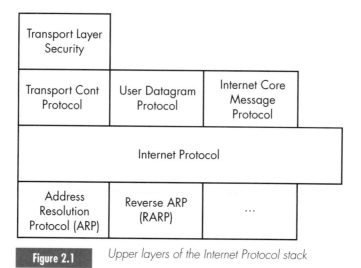

Transport Layer Security		
Transport Cont Protocol	User Datagram Protocol	Internet Core Message Protocol
Internet Protocol		
Address Resolution Protocol (ARP)	Reverse ARP (RARP)	...

Figure 2.1   *Upper layers of the Internet Protocol stack*

Directories use. For example, the services offered by the IP and the Internet Core Message Protocol (ICMP) are not directly used by Directory Services and so won't be discussed. However, an understanding of the TCP, Transport Layer Security (TLS, also known as Secure Sockets Layer or SSL), and the User Datagram Protocol (UDP) is directly used by Directory Services, and thus these terms will be introduced. However, before discussing these services specifically, it is important to understand how TCP/IP works so that the features that are available to the Directory are known.

The suite of protocols used by the Internet is known as the TCP/IP suite because the principal protocols that are used by Internet applications in order to communicate are the TCP and the IP. The TCP/IP suite of protocols is typically viewed as a stack, in which one layer is piled upon another. This is an indication that the layers at the top of the stack make use of services of the layers toward the bottom of the stack. Figure 2.1 shows a view of a portion of the TCP/IP stack.

In this figure, each layer in the stack provides a set of services that is available to the layers that reside logically on top of it. TLS directly makes use of the services provided by TCP but does not use any of the services that are offered by UDP or ICMP. Furthermore, TLS is generally ignorant of the services that are offered by the IP layer and does not directly make use of those services. Internet applications, such as Web Browsers, connect to Internet servers, such as Web Servers, by creating a connection known as a *socket* between the application and the server. A socket can be viewed as a pipeline between the application and the server through which data may be exchanged once it is created.

The creation of a socket is very analogous to the dialing of a telephone call. Once the telephone number is entered, the destination line rings; when the receiving party answers the ringing telephone on his or her end, a telephone connection is established. In order to create a socket connection between two entities on the Internet, the calling party (known as the client) enters an Internet address (the format of which will be discussed shortly). This Internet address is processed by a program running on the client's machine which attempts to make a connection to a program that is running on the machine named by the given Internet address. If there is any program listening for connections on the destination machine then the connection can be established. All of the Internet transports that are used in Internet Directories (i.e., TCP, UDP, and TLS) make use of sockets for communication between clients and servers but use different types of sockets. However, the sockets for all of the transport types have similar behavior. Thus, when they are used for the simple transport of data between the client and the server, the different socket types can be used by the Directory entities in virtually the same way.

During the attempt to create a socket, the client and server go through a process known as *handshaking*. During the handshaking process, the client and server each exchange some information before the socket can be created. If either side is not satisfied with the information that is provided by the other side (known as its peer) then the attempt to create the socket is broken off, and no socket connection is created. For example, a socket server may be configured in such a way that it allows sockets to be opened only by clients from a specified set of hosts. During the handshaking process the client and server exchange their address information. If the client's address is not one of those that the server is configured to accept then the server will reject the client's attempt to create the socket.

During any handshaking process at the Internet Transport Layer, the client and server exchange information in order that (among other things) they may be able to identify each other. In the real world, people identify each other by any number of means: for example, their names, their telephone numbers, their electronic mail addresses, and so forth. In the Internet, peer entities are able to identify each other by several different means, but by far the two most common mechanisms are Internet addresses and Internet host names. The following section presents an overview of the upper layers of the TCP/IP stack, from the top of the stack first, since those layers are directly used by the Directory.

The TLS Layer

A very simplified view of the handshaking that occurs in the TLS layer is shown in Figure 2.2. In this view of the handshaking that occurs during the attempt by a TLS client to open a socket with a TLS server, both the client and the server send two pieces of information across the network prior to a successful TLS socket creation. The client initiates the handshaking when it sends a special message defined by TLS, known as a *client hello*. This message contains various parameters that define those kinds of TLS services that are being requested. For example, the TLS client can request that the connection be encrypted by any of

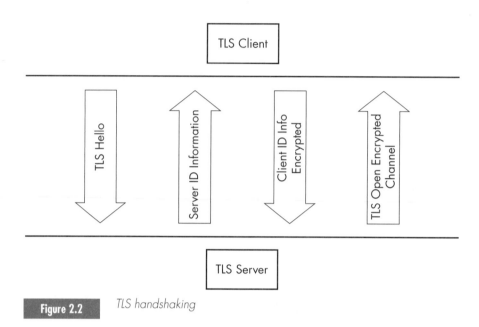

Figure 2.2   *TLS handshaking*

several different means. It can also request that any data being passed across the socket is to be compressed. The client hello message also includes some randomly generated data that aids in the creation of the encrypted connection. The server responds to a client hello with another special message that is defined by TLS, known as a *server hello*. The main piece of information included in the server hello message is information that is unique to the server, known as a certificate. The server presents its certificate in such a way that the client can verify that it really does belong to the server. This verification is known as *authentication*. The precise details of how this authentication works are not particularly important to the functions of Internet Directories, but a short overview of the authentication process will be discussed in Chapter 5 on Directory Management. The important feature of this first stage in the handshaking process is that it has allowed the TLS client to verify that the TLS server to which it has connected is indeed the one that it intended to contact.

Once the client has authenticated the server, the second phase of the TLS handshaking can begin. The objectives of the second phase are to allow the server to authenticate the client and to create an encryption key that allows all data passed across the TLS session to be kept confidential. If the server requested client authentication in its server hello message, then the client is obligated to provide its certificate information in the subsequent message. At this time the client uses the random data that it provided in the client hello message along with information that is in the server certificate to generate the encryption key. Simultaneous to this, the server is performing the same process, thus guaranteeing that the client and server have generated the same key, often known as a *shared secret*. If the server is satisfied with the client certificate information that the client has provided, then it provides a response that indicates that the connection has been opened successfully. Keep in mind that this explanation of TLS connection creation has been greatly simplified, and, while accurate, many details have been omitted.

The TCP Layer

TCP takes care of providing a reliable connection between two Internet nodes (e.g., hosts). For example, TCP nodes synchronize with each other and number each packet that is sent between them. For each packet that is sent from one host to the other, an acknowledgment is returned. If a host does not receive an acknowledgment for a sent packet, that packet is presumed to have been lost and is retransmitted. The TCP handshaking and socket setup process is much simpler than that of TLS. When a TCP client wishes to open with a TCP server, the client transmits a special message that indicates that it wishes to *synchronize* sequence numbers with the server. This message, known as a SYN message, is the first step in the TCP handshaking. The steps in the TCP handshaking are illustrated in Figure 2.3 (taken from RFC 793, which defines TCP).

RFC 793 describes this process, known as the *three-way handshake,* as follows: The TCP client begins by sending a SYN segment indicating that it will use sequence numbers starting with 100. Next, the TCP server sends a SYN and acknowledges the SYN it received from the TCP client. Note that the

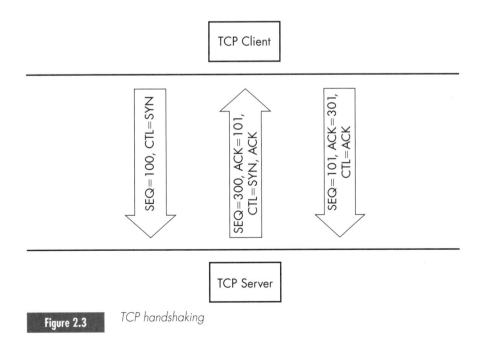

| **Figure 2.3** | *TCP handshaking* |

acknowledgment field indicates that the TCP server is now expecting to hear sequence 101, acknowledging the SYN, which occupied sequence 100. Finally, the TCP client responds with an empty segment containing an acknowledgment (ACK) for the TCP server's SYN. With this third message, the TCP client and server have successfully negotiated a socket connection.

The synchronizing of the TCP sequence numbers is particularly important to the reliability of the TCP layer. As RFC 793 indicates, TCP must recover data that is damaged, lost, duplicated, or delivered out of order by the IP layer. This is achieved by assigning a sequence number to each octet transmitted and requiring a positive ACK from the receiving TCP. If the ACK is not received within a timeout interval, the data is retransmitted. At the receiver, the sequence numbers are used to correctly order segments that may be received out of order and to eliminate duplicates. Damage is handled by adding a checksum to each segment transmitted, checking it at the receiver, and discarding damaged segments.

The UDP Layer

TCP is an inherently reliable protocol (using the above notion of reliability) because packets are sent again when lost or somehow damaged in transit. Its companion protocol UDP is considered to be an inherently unreliable protocol because the guarantees of TCP are not made by UDP. UDP does not recover from data that is damaged, lost, duplicated, or delivered out of order by the IP layer and does not have a handshaking process. UDP is designed for situations in which all that is needed is a single message and a single response. Thus, no ongoing connection between a UDP client and server is maintained. UDP is defined in RFC 768, which indicates that UDP provides a procedure for application programs to send messages to other programs with a minimum of protocol mechanisms. Applications requiring ordered reliable delivery of streams of data should use TCP. UDP operates by the UDP client opening a socket to a UDP server and sending some data across the socket. The UDP server replies to this request with whatever data is appropriate, and the UDP socket is then closed.

Tying the Layers Together

Most hosts that are reachable on the Internet have been assigned one or more Internet Protocol (IP) addresses and usually have been assigned a host name as well.[1] The IP is the numeric form, while the host name is the textual form. For convenience, the numeric addresses are normally represented textually in the

---

1. Modern techniques allow hosts to participate in the Internet without having an IP address (or host name) assigned to them.

dotted notation form, such as 127.0.0.1, rather than as the raw 32-bit or 64-bit number. Humans prefer the host name, as the names generally have some intrinsic meaning. For example, the Web site for the Prentice Hall publishing company is located on the Internet host *www.prenhall.com.* Host names are the text strings that appear on the right side of the "@" in electronic mail addresses. For example, the author can be reached via email at *bgreenblatt@directory-applications.com.*

Version 4 of IP, which is the current ubiquitously deployed version, allows for the IP address to be 32 bits, which is large enough to hold approximately four billion different addresses. The recently approved version 6 of IP allows for 64-bit addresses, which is large enough to hold over four quintillion (i.e., 4.6×10^{18}) addresses.

In addition to knowing the name or address of the server on which it wants to open a socket, the client must also know the number of the port to which the server is connected. To allow many processes within a single host to use TCP communication facilities simultaneously, the TCP provides a set of addresses or *ports* within each host. Concatenated with the network and host addresses from the IP layer, this forms a socket. This definition, taken directly from RFC 793, indicates that the purpose of the TCP port is to allow many servers to operate on the same Internet host at the same time. A TCP port is identified by an integer. In order to make this happen, each server must listen to a different incoming port. If a server attempts to listen on a port to which another server is already listening, TCP will return an error to the second server that indicates that the port is busy. Both UDP and TLS support the same implementation of port numbers, in that only one server is allowed to listen on a port at a time. Historically, Internet application services have reserved ports when they were defined. The Internet Assigned Numbers Authority (IANA) keeps track of all port numbers that have been assigned. Some of the more notable assignments for service contact ports are in Table 2.1.

Table 2.1	Port number assignments for some Internet Protocols		
Protocol Name	**TCP Port**	**UDP Port**	**TLS Port**
Telnet	23	23	992
SMTP−	25	25	465
DNS	53	53	—
Whois	43	43	—
Whois++	63	63	—
Finger	79	79	—
HTTP	80	80	443
LDAP	389	389	636
Rwhois	4,321	4,321	—

Note in Table 2.1 that not all Internet application protocols have been assigned TLS ports. Port numbers are divided into three separate ranges:

- Well-known ports, numbered from 0 through 1,023
- Registered ports, numbered from 1,024 through 49,151
- Dynamic or private ports, numbered from 49,152 through 65,535

Thus, DNS uses a well-known port, while Rwhois uses a registered port. The distinction between these two port types is minor, in that typically only processes or programs that are run by the most privileged users can listen on a well-known port number. If a service has a well-known or registered port assignment then clients of that service can assume that the default configuration of the server has the server listening on the assigned port. Thus, finger clients normally assume that there is a finger server listening on port number 79 on most Internet hosts and that there is never a server that doesn't understand the finger protocol listening on that port. This means that when the finger client attempts to open a socket to a finger server, it will try port 79, and it will both succeed and talk to a finger server, or there will not be a finger server active on that server. It will never be the case that the finger client will attempt to open the socket and that there is a server listening on port 79 that does not understand the finger protocol (for example, a Web server).

More information on the definition of the Internet may be found in the Internet document, FYI 20, entitled *What Is the Internet,* as well as any number of other published references.

Directories

Recall from our earlier discussion that a Directory is an application service that primarily performs property-based information retrieval. Directories store objects of various types. Each object that is stored has properties. For example, people objects have properties, such as given name, surname, email address, and so on. A Directory that contains objects of this type would allow clients to retrieve information about people based on the properties that have been defined.

As they relate to the Internet, Directories perform various necessary and useful functions. For example:

- They allow for the resolution of host names to underlying IP address.
- They allow for the creation of an Internet Public Key Infrastructure (PKI) in order to allow for the secure exchange of information across an insecure network.
- They allow for controlled access to resources across a distributed network.
- They allow for location of a server based upon the type of the service (e.g., electronic mail) rather than upon the name of the server.
- They allow for the exchange of index information among themselves in order to facilitate the routing of queries to the appropriate server. This

function allows each server to have some knowledge about the data that is contained on many other servers.

So, Directories provide many useful services for the Internet. But the Internet also provides many useful functions for Directories. TCP provides a reliable means of transporting data from client to server. TLS allows for the Directory to provide a secure means of transporting data from client to server. TLS also allows the Directory peers to provide a strong means of identifying each other rather than simply passing user IDs and passwords across the network.

The previous section provided an overview of the Internet, and the notion of Directories as a service that allows for property-based information retrieval has been touched upon. Putting the Internet and Directories together yields the concept of the Internet Directory. *An Internet Directory is a service that has property-based information retrieval as its primary function and uses one or more of the Internet transports (TLS, TCP, or UDP) as its native means for communication between the client and server.* The two most prominent Internet Directories are the Domain Name Service (DNS) and the LDAP.

LDAP

The LDAP was defined as a result of ARPA's desire to pursue implementation of the X.500 series of recommendations of the International Telecommunications Union (X.500). X.500 defines several different models and protocols that are used in the implementation of Directories. The most notable protocol defined by X.500 is the Directory Access Protocol (DAP). ARPA wanted to deploy Directories based on the X.500 series, but their implementation was slow in coming. ARPA decided to fund a research project at the University of Michigan that would result in the definition of a different version of DAP that would be significantly easier to implement but would still retain the core features of the X.500 model. The end product of this research project was LDAP.

An early definition of LDAP was experimental in nature, and the first widely implemented definition of LDAP was LDAP version 2 as defined in RFC 1777. Because of deficiencies in the areas of security, internationalization, and extensibility, a third version of LDAP was defined in RFC 2251, which indicates that key aspects of this version of LDAP are the following:

- All features of LDAP version 2 (RFC 1777) are supported. The protocol is carried directly over TCP or other transport, bypassing much of the session/presentation overhead of X.500 DAP (which is defined on top of the OSI protocol stack).
- Most of the data that is passed between LDAP clients and servers can be encoded as ordinary strings (X.500 uses various binary data types to encode its information).

- Referrals to other servers may be returned when the server that was initially contacted by the LDAP client does not have enough information in order to completely fulfill the client request.
- Any mechanism may be used with LDAP to provide security services that can be used in the authentication step between the client and the server.
- Attribute values and Distinguished Names have been internationalized to allow for any character (e.g., in the Chinese character set) to be used in LDAP strings.
- The protocol can be extended to support new operations, and controls may be used to extend existing operations.
- Clients publish schemas in the Directory for use, so that the types of information that are available for retrieval are part and parcel of the normal information published by LDAP servers.

The last point is especially interesting. In the context of Internet Directories, the schema defines the types of objects and the properties of those objects that are available for retrieval by clients. Since LDAP clients are the ones that are capable of publishing the information that appears in Directories, it is only natural that the clients are allowed to publish (and retrieve) the schema for that information. While appearing natural, this innovation is new in version 3 of LDAP and allows clients to be able to find out about new types of objects that are stored in the Directory and to determine the precise syntax that is used in the properties of these new types of objects.

In the previous sections of this chapter, various functions of Internet Directories have been discussed, but the fundamental requirements for a Directory service have only been touched on. In traditional software development, the requirements-gathering phase is the first part of developing software, and it defines the external behavior of the software system to be built. In terms of Internet Directories, the requirements indicate the features of the clients that are made available to their users. Note that not all Directory services implement all of these requirements. For example, as mentioned previously, DNS does not implement schema discovery. This section is meant to describe, in a general way, the types of features that are available in many Internet Directory services in order to distinguish them from other types of application services.

The foremost requirement of an Internet Directory service is to allow for property-based information retrieval. Regardless of the type of information that is stored in the Directory, each object that is stored has various properties, and the Directory service must allow for clients to retrieve this information based on these properties.

Data Storage

Internet Directories store their data in such a way that the properties and protocol that are used fit in naturally with the rest of the Internet. For example, multimedia objects are typically represented in the Internet by using the MIME structure. MIME stands for Multipurpose Internet Mail Extensions and was first defined as a way to transport various types of binary data across the Internet in electronic mail messages. However, the term has come to be used in numerous protocols that need to define ways to transport multipart, possibly binary data. For example, MIME is used not only in electronic mail but also in LDAP, the Common Index Protocol (CIP), the Hypertext Transport Protocol (HTTP) that is used in the World Wide Web, and many other Internet application protocols.

In the original days of the Internet, data was assumed to be stored in the United States (U.S.) version of the ASCII character set. U.S. ASCII represents each character as a single byte, the high-order bit of which is always zero. The resulting 128 different characters that are defined by U.S. ASCII include the 26 upper and lowercase letters, the 10 digits, and various other punctuation and control characters. Of course, information that is transported across the Internet needs to include characters from many different cultures outside the United States. For example, European and Asian characters are not represented in U.S. ASCII. The French word "çiel" can't be represented using U.S. ASCII, since the character "ç" is not one of the 128 characters defined by ASCII. In order to represent such kinds of information, the Universal Character Set (UCS) repertoire was devised. UCS character sequences are normally represented on the Internet by using the specification known as UTF-8. UTF-8 is defined in RFC 2279, which is titled, *UTF-8, A Transformation Format of ISO 10646.* The International Organization for Standardization (ISO) standard numbered 10646 defines the multibyte character set known as UCS. UCS characters are either two bytes long or four bytes long, and they use the full range of possible two or four byte values.

The point of UTF-8 is that it encodes UCS characters as a sequence of one or more 8-bit ASCII characters. UTF-8 defines an encoding mechanism that has the characteristic of preserving the full U.S. ASCII range. It also provides a mechanism for encoding characters outside of this range in more than one byte. Table 2.2 (taken directly from RFC 2279) summarizes the format of these different octet types. The letter "x" indicates bits available for encoding bits of the UCS-4 character value.

Table 2.2   *UTF-8 character encoding*

UCS-4 Range (hex.)	UTF-8 Octet Sequence (binary)	Number of 8-Bit Characters Needed
0000 0000-0000 007F	0xxxxxxx	1
0000 0080-0000 07FF	110xxxxx 10xxxxxx	2
0000 0800-0000 FFFF	1110xxxx 10xxxxxx 10xxxxxx	3
0001 0000-001F FFFF	11110xxx 10xxxxxx 10xxxxxx 10xxxxxx	4
0020 0000-03FF FFFF	111110xx 10xxxxxx 10xxxxxx 10xxxxxx 10xxxxxx	5
0400 0000-7FFF FFFF	1111110x 10xxxxxx . . . 10xxxxxx	6

Thus, the UTF-8 encoding of the word "Directory" is precisely the same as the original ASCII encoding of that same word. Some other examples from RFC 2279 of character encoding are:

1. The UCS-2 sequence "A<NOT IDENTICAL TO><ALPHA>" (0041, 2262, 0391, 002E) may be encoded in UTF-8 as follows: 41 E2 89 A2 CE 91 2E

2. The UCS-2 sequence representing the Hangul characters for the Korean word "hangugo" (D55C, AD6D, C5B4) may be encoded as follows: ED 95 9C EA B5 AD EC 96 B4

3. The UCS-2 sequence representing the Han characters for the Japanese word "nihongo" (65E5, 672C, 8A9E) may be encoded as follows: E6 97 A5 E6 9C AC E8 AA 9E

Since UTF-8 encoding is the Internet Standards track definition for international character representations, when representing data outside of the U.S.-ASCII character set, Internet Directories should make use of UTF-8 encoding for that data, as specified in RFC 2279.

Protocol Usage

The protocol used in LDAP is carried directly on top of an Internet Transport, such as TCP, UDP, or TLS. Native integration of applications with the TCP/IP stack makes integration with future enhancements to this stack more likely to be smooth. For example, TLS has been designed in such a way that creation and deletion of TLS sockets are done in virtually the same way as the creation and deletion of TCP sockets. For example, even though TLS had not yet been invented at the time that LDAP version 2 was released, LDAP version 2 clients have no problem in changing from the use of TCP to access Directory servers to using TLS to access those same Directory servers. LDAP version 2 clients thereby gained the advantage of encrypted sessions, server authentication, and other TLS-provided services without any change at all in the LDAP protocol definition.

Distributed Operation

An LDAP Directory operates in a distributed manner in such a way as to allow consistent access to their information throughout the Internet. Not all Internet hosts are uniformly available from any site on the Internet. This is due to a wide variety of factors, not the least of which are geographic considerations and other bandwidth-related concerns. However, access to Directory information should not suffer from these problems. It must be possible to allow multiple Directory servers to provide services for the same set of objects. This allows Directory clients to access whichever Directory server is most conveniently located. Figure 2.4 illustrates this requirement.

The point here is that any of the clients can present their query ("What people named 'smith' have a salary of over $50,000?") to any of the servers and expect to get the same answer back. Because of geographical and other band-

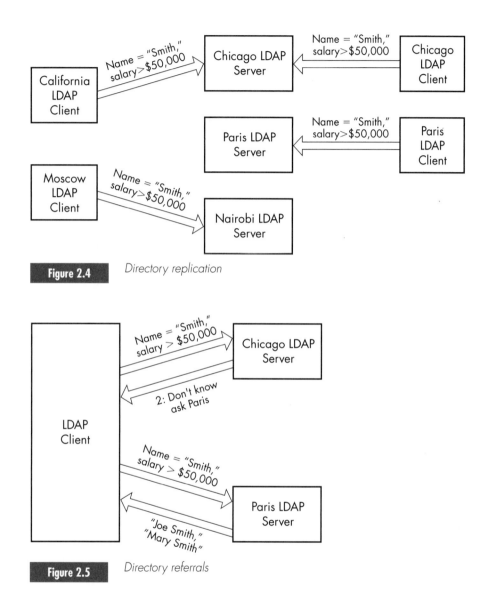

Figure 2.4   *Directory replication*

Figure 2.5   *Directory referrals*

width considerations, the timing will be different for each of the clients work-ing with each of the servers. Therefore, LDAP servers are required to cooperate in order to present a uniform view to Internet Directory Clients of the data that they manage. Historically, LDAP Servers that do support the notion of infor-mation sharing or replication have defined their own information-sharing pro-tocols that are specific to one type of Directory (e.g., NDS, Active Directory).

Because Directory servers cooperate to provide a service, if they are not able to fulfill a client request, they may be able to refer the client to another Di-rectory server. Figure 2.5 illustrates this notion of *referrals*.

In this figure the Directory client first submits its query about people named Smith with relatively decent salaries to the Chicago Directory server. The Chicago Directory server is unable to fulfill this request and refers the Directory client to the Paris Directory server. The Directory client *chases* the referral that is provided and presents the same query to the Paris Directory server. In this instance, the Paris Directory server is able to fulfill the client's request and furnishes an appropriate response. Thus, a referral is an indication by a Directory server that it does not have the information needed to return that desired result. The referral contains that information needed by the Directory client for it to be able to contact some other Directory server. Directories can gather knowledge of the information that is held by other Directory servers. The Directory administrator can manually gather this knowledge, or it can be automated by the use of Back End Directory Protocols.

White Pages Service

One of the main uses for a Directory on the Internet is to provide an Internet White Pages Service (IWPS). A white pages service is a service in which the client furnishes some properties of a user that it knows about, and the service responds with various types of address information about the user whose properties were supplied. In the context of the telephone system, clients will often use a white pages book, which lists names alphabetically. If the white pages client knows the name of a listed telephone subscriber, then the white pages service will supply the client with a telephone number and possibly a street address. An IWPS, as a special type of white pages service that is located on the Internet, is intended to provide Internet-related addressing information. In the IWPS, the principal addressing information that is to be returned by the IWPS server is the electronic mail address of a user. Other types of related information can also be returned. For instance, RFC 2148 *(Deployment of the Internet White Pages Service)* describes in great detail the requirements for an IWPS, and RFC 2218 *(A Common Schema for the Internet White Pages Service)* defines the data that is to be maintained by an IWPS server. A small subset of the user properties that RFC 2218 defines is

- Email
- Certificate
- Home Page
- Given Name
- Surname
- Organization
- Country
- Personal Phone
- Personal Fax

In the preceding list it can be seen that some of the properties are ones that the IWPS client generally provides in a request (e.g., Given Name, Surname, Country) while the IWPS server generally provides others in its response (e.g., Email, Certificate, Personal Phone). For example, an IWPS client in a search for someone's electronic mail address could provide:

- Given Name = "John"
- Surname = "Smith"
- Organization = "Prentice Hall"

While the IWPS server would respond with *john.smith@prenhall.com.* An IWPS was historically connected with electronic mail packages and often called an Address Book service. Many people confuse an IWPS with the Directory service itself. This important distinction is made between a service and an application of that service. The Directory service is a general-purpose property-based information retrieval service, while an IWPS is a special purpose service optimized for retrieval of user's addressing properties.

Chapter Summary

This chapter provided a general-purpose definition of a Directory as a *property-based information retrieval system.* This definition will be used throughout the book. The simple example of a White Pages Directory Service was given. Additionally, the various upper layers of the Internet protocol stack were defined. Finally, this chapter gave a quick overview of LDAP. With this foundation of computer networking, as well as a quick overview of some Directories and their applications, we can progress into more detailed definitions in the chapters to come.

LDAP Overview

CHAPTER OBJECTIVES

In order to explain adequately the appropriate ways to write LDAP applications that work with Active Directory and NDS, we must first have a solid background in LDAP itself. The LDAP specification includes the definition of the data that is transferred across a TCP/IP network between an LDAP client and an LDAP server. This protocol defines the means by which the client can create, modify, and retrieve data that is stored at the server. LDAP also defines a logical organization of the data. This logical organization of the data is sometimes called the information model. LDAP does not define a physical layout of the data. NDS and Active Directory servers use different storage strategies. The actual storage mechanism is transparent to the LDAP programmer. The programmer can retrieve and manipulate the stored information using LDAP irrespective of the actual storage mechanism. This chapter will explain the different operations that are available in LDAP. It will also provide an overview of the LDAP information model.

LDAP is an attempt by the IETF to create a standard protocol for accessing directories that are designed in the manner of the X.500 series or recommendations of the International Telecommunications Union (ITU).[1] The ITU, a standards body that is a division of the United Nations, concentrates on standardizing communications that are to take place between and among various public telecommunications administrations and government postal authorities.

The X.500 series of recommendations was originally defined in the period from 1985 to 1988. Its original requirements were to provide features to better enable the ITU's X.400 series of recommendations for electronic mail. Among other items, X.500 provided the strong authentication features for communications between clients and servers, as well as the ability for location-independent addressing of electronic mail. Addressing based on X.500 Directory names was an attempt to address the dilemma of complex X.400 address formats. Unfortunately, the naming provided by the X.500 information model is not significantly simpler than that provided by X.400. Since its original definition in 1988, the X.500 series has been revised and extended several times to fix implementation errors and has provided additional features. X.500-based Directory services never gained significant presence in the market for a variety of reasons, not the least of which was X.500's reliance upon the existence of an OSI protocol stack at a time when most network operating systems did not offer such a service natively.

In order to make the X.500 style of directories more available, the IETF began standardization efforts that led to the development of LDAP. LDAP derives its name from the X.500 client-server protocol, DAP. The first version of LDAP was defined in RFC 1487. A second version was defined in RFC 1777. LDAP version 2 was the first version that was widely implemented. The definition of the third version of LDAP in RFC 2251 improves upon the previous version by adding better support for international character sets, providing for additional security support, allowing for distributed commands, and providing for extensions to the protocol. LDAP tries to remove some of the complexities of implementing DAP by

- Mapping directly onto the transport layer of the TCP/IP stack,
- Encoding many elements of the protocol as strings, and
- Using a more lightweight version of the OSI "basic encoding rules."

Thus, LDAP makes use of the TCP/IP stack rather than the OSI stack. One concept that LDAP borrows from the OSI world involves the OSI basic encoding rules, which are part of a feature of the presentation layer of the OSI model known as Abstract Syntax Notation One (ASN.1). ASN.1 is the ITU's mechanism

---

1. ITU documents are known as Recommendations. They are normally named with a letter and a number. An entire series of related recommendations are numbered closely together to form a series. The recommendations X.400, X.401, X.402, etc., are all related to electronic mail and are known collectively as the X.400 series. Similarly, X.500, X.501, X.509, etc., are all related to directories and are known collectively as the X.500 series.

for defining the language that its peer entities use to communicate across a data communications network. ASN.1 and its associated encoding rules define not only the type of data that is used in communications but also the mapping of the data layouts into the binary network order.

Even though ASN.1 is used to encode the LDAP information that is transferred between the client and server, in most instances, the LDAP application programmer never is aware of ASN.1. This is due to the fact that the popular APIs hide the details of the ASN.1 encoding and decoding from the programmer. Thus, this chapter will not define LDAP in terms of its actual protocol but instead will define the semantics of the available LDAP client commands and the possible server replies.

LDAP Namespace and Information Model

The information that is available via LDAP is organized in a hierarchical manner. In DNS, each entry in the Directory is named by a hostname. In LDAP, each entry in the Directory is given a special name, known as the distinguished name (or simply the entry's DN). Figure 3.1 illustrates an example of the hierarchy used in LDAP.

The collection of all entries in an LDAP hierarchy is called the Directory Information Tree (DIT). In LDAP, in order to form the DN of an entry in the DIT, one starts from the bottom of the hierarchy and works toward the top. A comma separates each name component. Each component of the DN is called the Relative Distinguished Name (RDN). So, the sales organizational unit at the bottom of Figure 3.1 would have the distinguished name:

OU=Sales, O=Acme, C=US

Each LDAP server has information about some set of distinguished names that are organized in a hierarchical manner. LDAP assumes that the combination of the hostname and distinguished name uniquely identifies an entry in the Directory. Thus, two different Directory servers might maintain two different entries with the same distinguished name. This can cause problems if the two LDAP servers are connected and they attempt to synchronize their information. This points out the need for a registration process in order to avoid naming collisions. Many organizations base the top level of their LDAP hierarchies on the DNS names that they have registered. In fact, the naming scheme imposed by the Active Directory enforces this DNS-based naming scheme. However, no problems arise as long as the LDAP servers are allowed to maintain their own information.

In LDAP it has been common practice for administrators to set up the top of the namespace themselves, and they have had substantial freedom to do so.

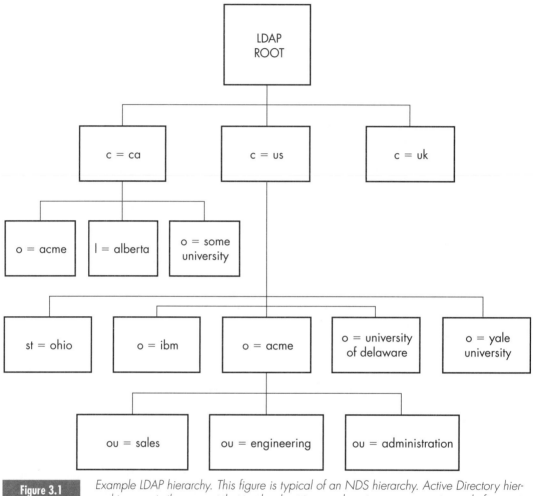

Figure 3.1   *Example LDAP hierarchy. This figure is typical of an NDS hierarchy. Active Directory hierarchies are similar, except that top-level entries are domain components instead of countries or organizations.*

For example, in the United States, NDS LDAP trees will be rooted with the single entry named by the distinguished name, "C=US." In this name, the "C" is the abbreviation for the attribute: countryName. The entry identified by a country-Name attribute is a country entry. This entry has other attributes besides its name. For example, it is allowed to have a description. There is no universal guarantee that the description that is present in the "C=US" entry on one Directory server will also be present on some other Directory server. In this instance, nothing bad happens just because my "C=US" entry is not the same as your "C=US" entry.

Active Directory uses a different naming scheme. This naming scheme is based on the DNS hierarchy and will be explained in detail in Chapter 6.

In LDAP, each entry is allowed to logically contain other entries. Placing one entry beneath another in the hierarchy represents this containment notion. So far, we've seen two different kinds of entries: the country entry and the organization entry, although admittedly in very little detail. Now, a few LDAP entries will be examined in more detail.

An *object class* identifies each kind of entry that is stored in LDAP. An object class definition is made up of several items:

- The name of the object class
- The name of the super class
- The list of mandatory attributes of this object class
- The list of optional attributes of this object class
- The type of object class, ABSTRACT, STRUCTURAL, or AUXILIARY

The attributes of an object class are divided into those that must be in every object (the mandatory ones) and those that are in some entries of that class but are missing from other entries of that class (the optional ones). The most basic LDAP object class, "Top," is the only LDAP object class that does not have a superclass. All other LDAP object classes are descended from Top. The Top object class has the following definition (as taken from RFC 2256):

```
( 2.5.6.0 NAME 'top' ABSTRACT MUST objectClass )
```

This LDAP object class definition indicates that the object class named Top has exactly one mandatory attribute named *objectClass*. The object class Top does not have any optional attributes, since they are not mentioned in the definition. Since a superclass is also absent, the object class Top does not have one. The keyword ABSTRACT in the definition of Top indicates that no actual entries of that type may be created. The Top object class may be used only in the definition of other object classes. Since no Top entries can be created, the question of naming them does not arise, but the components of an object's distinguished name are normally composed from the mandatory attributes. RFC 2256 contains the "User Schema" for use in LDAP. It defines numerous common object classes and attribute types that form the foundation for the NDS and Active Directory schemas.

The dotted numeric identifier at the beginning of the object class definition is another way of representing the name of the object class. In this case, the name "Top" and the numeric identifier "2.5.6.0" both refer to the same thing, that is, the object class named Top. These numeric identifiers, known as object identifiers (OIDs), are encoded as the character string representation, and that is how they appear in the protocol. Each OID is universally unique. Thus, no matter where the OID "2.5.6.0" appears, it always refers to the object class named Top. These OIDs have been assigned as part of the X.500 recommendations.

Normally, in LDAP the numeric identifier for the object class name is not used, and the textual name is used. This is because in LDAP, an OID can appear in the protocol as either the descriptive form or the numeric form. Since people greatly prefer to see the descriptive form, that is what is commonly used.

Top's sole attribute, objectClass attribute, is defined as

```
( 2.5.4.0 NAME 'objectClass' EQUALITY objectIdentifierMatch
     SYNTAX 1.3.6.1.4.1.1466.115.121.1.38 )
```

The OID for the objectClass attribute is "2.5.4.0." The next part of the attribute definition identifies the type of matching rules that can be used in LDAP searches. In this case, LDAP searches can be performed only for exact equality against objectClass attributes. So, an LDAP search could be performed in order to retrieve all entries that were of the type "person." But, an LDAP search to retrieve all entries that had an objectClass attribute greater than "person" would be illegal, since only the EQUALITY matching rule is allowed.

The last portion of the attribute definition describes the syntax of the attribute values. The syntax describes the format of the attribute values as they are transferred across the LDAP connection. Most LDAP attribute values use the string syntax. This numeric identifier is another OID, as defined in RFC 2252, which in this case indicates that the syntax is of type "OID." Remember that in LDAP, the OID syntax refers to either the numeric identifier form or the textual description form, and that in the case of the objectClass attribute, the textual format is nearly always used.

The next object classes that will be examined are the organization object class and the organizationalUnit object class. These two similar object classes will be used to define the top-level containers in the example Directory tree later in this chapter. They have virtually identical definitions in RFC 2256, as shown here:

```
( 2.5.6.4 NAME 'organization' SUP top STRUCTURAL
MUST o MAY ( userPassword $ searchGuide $ seeAlso $
businessCategory $ x121Address $ registeredAddress $
destinationIndicator $ preferredDeliveryMethod $
telexNumber $ teletexTerminalIdentifier $ telephoneNumber
$ internationaliSDNNumber $ facsimileTelephoneNumber $
street $ postOfficeBox $ postalCode $ postalAddress $
physicalDeliveryOfficeName $ st $ l $ description ) )

( 2.5.6.5 NAME 'organizationalUnit' SUP top STRUCTURAL
MUST ou MAY ( userPassword $ searchGuide $ seeAlso $
businessCategory $ x121Address $ registeredAddress $
destinationIndicator $ preferredDeliveryMethod $
telexNumber $ teletexTerminalIdentifier $ telephoneNumber
$ internationaliSDNNumber $ facsimileTelephoneNumber $
street $ postOfficeBox $ postalCode $ postalAddress $
physicalDeliveryOfficeName $ st $ l $ description ) )
```

These two object class definitions are significantly longer than the definition of the abstract class Top. Notice that the only difference in the two definitions is that the organization object class has a mandatory attribute named "o" and the organizationalUnit object class has a mandatory attribute named "ou." In these object class definitions, the superclass field is present, which indicates that both are derived from the class Top. When one object class is a superclass of another class (the subclass), this means that the subclass has all of the mandatory and optional attributes of the superclass. So, in addition to all of the attributes mentioned, all organization and organizationalUnit entries in the Directory will also have an objectClass attribute. One final object class from RFC 2256 that will be used to populate entries in the sample Directory is the one that is used to represent people entries in the Directory. This is the person object class:

```
( 2.5.6.6 NAME 'person' SUP top STRUCTURAL MUST ( sn $ cn )
   MAY ( userPassword $ telephoneNumber $ seeAlso $
   description ) )
```

In this object class, both the surname attribute (sn) and the common name attribute (cn) must be present, in addition to the objectClass attribute that is inherited from the top object class. The LDAP protocol expects the cn attribute to be used in the formation of the DN of the Directory object representing that person. In organizational directories, the cn is often used to hold an employee identification number. Note also that LDAP allows an entry's cn attribute to have more than one value. Not all of the cn values need to be unique identifiers in the Directory context. For example, the cn attribute is also often used to hold a user identifier for authentication to the network. Note that the current version of Active Directory does not allow the cn attribute to be multivalued. Subsequent versions of Active Directory are expected to remedy this deficiency.

This notion of multivalued attributes is common throughout LDAP. For example, any person object that appears in the Directory will have two values of the objectClass attribute: *person* and *top*. This is very analogous to the situation in Domain Name System (DNS) in which the same Internet host may have several valid names. In other words, it is possible for the two hostnames *mail.acme.com* and *news.acme.com* to refer to the same IP address. In LDAP it is possible for two common names to refer to the same underlying Directory entry or to many different entries. With these object class definitions, enough information is in place in order to begin to set up the structure of the example Directory.

In Figure 3.2, the boxes with the diagonal line shading represent organizationalUnit entries, the boxes with the vertical line shading represent person entries, and the unshaded object represents the top-level Internet organization object. In this example, the Directory content consists of ten entries: four organizationalUnits, five person entries, and one organization. The entries in Figure 3.2 are represented only by their RDNs, but they may have other attributes associated with that entry. Consider the "US breeders" organizationalUnit in Table 3.1.

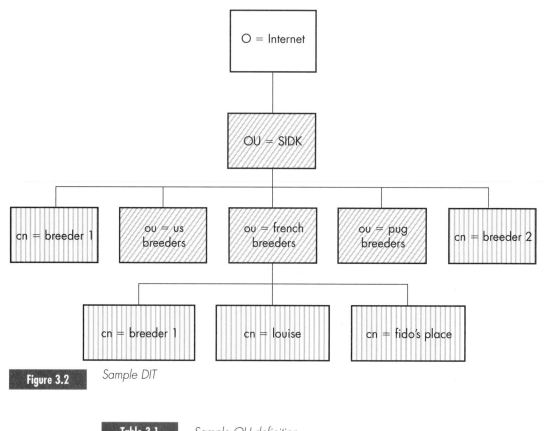

Figure 3.2   *Sample DIT*

Table 3.1	*Sample OU definition*
Attribute Type	**Attribute Value(s)**
OU	"US Breeders,"
	"United States Breeders"
ObjectClass	"top," "organizationalUnit"
Description	"Dog breeders that are located in the United States of America"
SeeAlso	"ou=American Breeders, o=Internet"

In this entry, both values for the mandatory attributes of the object class are present. The mandatory nature of the objectClass attribute is inherited from the superclass, "Top." In addition, it has the mandatory attribute "ou" from the definition of the organizationalUnit object class. Notice that there are multiple values for each of these two mandatory attributes. Notice also that of the numerous available optional attributes for the organizationalUnit object class, only two are present in this entry. The entry has a description attribute present, as well as a seeAlso attribute. The description attribute contains a short textual overview of the purpose of the entry. In this case, the description attribute indicates that the entry contains information about dog breeders located in the United States. The seeAlso attribute indicates that a somewhat-related entry is the entry denoted by the DN "ou=American Breeders, o=Internet." Unfortunately, the seeAlso attribute doesn't indicate the nature of the relationship between the entries, only that there is one. Consider the "fido's place" person entry in Table 3.2.

Table 3.2	*Sample person object*
Attribute Type	**Attribute Value(s)**
CN	"fido's place,"
	"acme dog breeding, inc.,"
	"SN: 032861"
ObjectClass	"top," "person"
TelephoneNumber	"1234-12-12," "fax: 0912203993"
Description	"World-renowned breeders of canine-type animals,"
	"We also breed cats, but don't tell anyone"

Note the similar nature of the attributes between this entry and the previous example, "ou=us breeders, o=Internet." An important item to note is that even though the object class is person, the entry obviously does not represent a person. It clearly represents a company of some sort that breeds dogs and (judging from the second value of the description attribute) cats.

One obvious flaw in the design of the Information Structure for this Directory is that the available object classes or attributes have little to do with breeding dogs. This is not surprising, as it is the intent of the definitions RFC 2256 to provide the starting point for definitions, and numerous other object classes and attributes will likely be defined in the future by various special interest groups. Indeed, the IETF itself has already defined a schema for the support of an Internet White Pages Services (IWPS). The IWPS schema is intended to provide most of the information about people that would likely be used in searches. This schema, defined in RFC 2218, indicates that an object class that is defined to hold information about Internet users should have the information shown in Figure 3.3.

Field Name, Email, Cert, Home Page, Common Name, Given Name, Surname, Organization, Locality, Country, Language Spoken, Personal Phone, Personal Fax, Personal Mobile, Personal Pager Number, Personal Postal Address, Description, Title, Office Phone, Office Fax, Office Mobile Phone, Office Pager, Office Postal Address

Figure 3.3   *Proposed attributes for an IWPS user*

RFC 2218 doesn't define an LDAP object class, it just mentions the kinds of information that an LDAP object class should hold.

In order to illustrate the information structure of LDAP, let's consider the example of a Directory that contains information about breeds of dogs. Presume that the "Society of Internet Dog Kennels," or SIDK, maintains this Directory. The administrator has chosen to use the "O=Internet" entry as the root of its Directory tree. It would be inappropriate to place the entry representing the SIDK organization underneath any particular country entry, since the dog breeds and breeders are located throughout the world.

In addition to the IWPS style information, the example Directory needs to hold the kind of information that is specific to the breeders of dogs that populate the SIDK organization's DIT. In order for this type of information to be present in the Directory, two additional object classes will be defined: *breeder* and *breedingOrganization.* In defining these additional object classes, a significant decision must be made. They can be defined as either structural subclasses of object classes that are already defined or as auxiliary object classes.

An auxiliary object class is one that can be added to an existing entry in the Directory in such a way that the additional attributes defined in the auxiliary object class are added to the object. This is very similar to the use of the subclass, except that an entry's auxiliary object classes can change over time. LDAP allows an entry to only ever have one base structural object class, and if this needs to change, then the entry must be deleted from the Directory and subsequently added to the Directory again with a new object class. This is a dangerous thing to do, since all references to the old entry may be damaged (or even deleted) when the entry is destroyed. So, it is safer for the SIDK organization to define its private information as auxiliary object classes.

For the goals here, the definition of valid OIDs serves no real purpose, so it will be omitted. The breeder object class has the following definition:

```
(NAME 'breeder' SUP top AUXILIARY MUST ( breed $
emailAddress )

    MAY ( homePage $ givenName $ postalAddress $
    breedersOrganization ) )
```

In this definition, some of the attributes from RFC 2218 have been selected. Additionally, several attribute definitions that are unique to the SIDK organization have been defined, since there is no IETF standardized definition for them. So, we'll supply definitions for breed and breedersOrganization:

```
(NAME 'breed' EQUALITY caseIgnoreMatch

    SUBSTR caseIgnoreSubstringsMatch

    SYNTAX 1.3.6.1.4.1.1466.115.121.1.15{64} )

(NAME 'breedersOrganization' EQUALITY
distinguishedNameMatch

    SYNTAX 1.3.6.1.4.1.1466.115.121.1.12 SINGLE-VALUE )
```

These definitions require a little explanation. When a client performs LDAP searches, the breed attribute may be found by supplying either the entire string (an EQUALITY match) or only part of the string (a SUBSTR, i.e., substring match). The OID that is given after the SYNTAX keyword is defined in RFC 2252 indicates that breed attributes are defined using the DirectoryString syntax. An attribute that is encoded using the DirectoryString syntax is a character string that is encoded in the UTF-8 representation of the Unicode character set. Unicode is a special character set in which virtually any character that is used in human communication can be represented by either two bytes or four bytes. The UTF-8 representation (defined in RFC 2044) is a special transformation of the Unicode representation into a special representation in which some characters are represented using only a single byte, while other characters may be represented by as many as six bytes. Unicode characters that also appear in the seven-bit ASCII character set are represented by one byte in the UTF-8 transformation. Other Unicode characters are represented in UTF-8 depending upon their Unicode representation. Table 3.3 gives an example of RFC 2253, which defines the UTF-8 String Representation of Distinguished Names.

Table 3.3	Sample UTF-8 string		
Unicode Letter Description	**10646 code**	**UTF-8**	**Quoted**
Latin capital letter L	U0000004C	0x4C	L
Latin small letter U	U00000075	0x75	U
Latin small letter C with caron	U0000010D	0xC48D	\C4\8D
Latin small letter I	U00000069	0x69	I
Latin small letter C with acute	U00000107	0xC487	\C4\87

These five characters could be written in printable ASCII (useful for debugging purposes):

```
Lu\C4\8Di\C4\87
```

Notice that the ASCII characters L, u, and i have the same representation in UTF-8 as they do in the standard ASCII representation. The other two characters that don't appear in ASCII, but are in Unicode, require two bytes per character. The backslash ("\") character is used to indicate Unicode characters that are outside of the normal ASCII character set. Two ASCII characters that indicate the Unicode character follow each backslash character. The backslash character used in the quoted version does not appear in the protocol. The bytes listed in the UTF-8 column of Table 3.3 appear. Thus seven bytes are required to represent the five-character string. This definition of the breed attribute allows it to hold dog breed names that contain characters outside of ASCII. The breedersOrganization attribute allows the breeder object to contain the distinguished name of an organization that has sanctioned this breeder. Notice that this attribute has the keyword SINGLE-VALUE present. This indicates that there may only be one value of this attribute present in the object. So, while each breeder may have several breed values present in the Directory object, it may have only one breedersOrganization attribute value present. Note that if this restriction didn't make sense in the real-world representation of the data to be contained in the Directory, then the SINGLE-VALUE restriction should be dropped from the attribute definition.

Now that the breed object class has been defined, the breedingOrganization must be specified as well:

```
(NAME 'breedingOrganization' SUP top AUXILIARY MUST
( breed $ emailAddress ) MAY ( homePage $ contactUser
$ postalAddress) )
```

This requires the additional definition of the contactUser:

```
(NAME 'contactUser' EQUALITY distinguishedNameMatch
   SYNTAX 1.3.6.1.4.1.1466.115.121.1.12 )
```

The contactUser attribute of the breedingOrganization gives the distinguished names of some users that can be contacted as representatives of the organization. Notice that while the breedingOrganization object class has the breed attribute just as the breeder object class does, each class has slightly different semantics in each definition. When used in the breeder object class, the breed attribute is intended to represent the types of breeds of dogs that the breeder breeds. When used in the breedingOrganization object class, the breed attribute is intended to represent the types of breeds of dogs that can be shown in the dog shows that this organization officially sanctions. With these object class and attribute definitions, the example DIT entries can now be updated (see Tables 3.4 and 3.5).

Table 3.4	Sample OU entry updated
Attribute Type	**Attribute Value(s)**
OU	"US Breeders,"
	"United States Breeders"
ObjectClass	"top," "organizationalUnit," "breedingOrganization"
Description	"Dog breeders that are located in the United States of America"
SeeAlso	"ou=American Breeders, o=Internet"
Breed	"pug," "poodle," "beagle," "irish setter"
EmailAddress	"*info@usbreeders.org*"
Homepage	"*www.usbreeders.org*"
ContactUser	"cn=alice, ou=us breeders, o=Internet"

Table 3.5	*Sample Person entry updated*
Attribute Type	**Attribute Value(s)**
CN	"fido's place,"
	"acme dog breeding, inc.,"
	"SN: 032861"
ObjectClass	"top," "person," "breeder"
TelephoneNumber	"1234-12-12," "fax: 0912203993"
Description	"World-renowned breeders of canine-type animals,"
	"We also breed cats, but don't tell anyone"
Breed	"pug"
EmailAddress	*"Fido@fidosplace.fr"*
Homepage	*"www.fidosplace.fr"*

Notice how these entries have been filled out with more information that is appropriate to the SIDK organization's Directory, instead of the simple generic person and organizational attributes that are supplied by the base LDAP object class definitions. In the entries, there is no way for the LDAP client to determine whether the breeder object class is auxiliary or structural. If the breeder object class were defined as structural subclass of the person object class there would be no difference in the definition of the attributes of the entries. Thus, there is no real reason that the LDAP client implementation needs to know whether any particular object class is structural or auxiliary when reading entries from the Directory. However, as was mentioned before, the only values of the objectClass attribute that can be changed are the auxiliary ones. The base structural attribute value of an object in the Directory can never be changed. This restriction is specified in the X.500 series of recommendations and is carried over as a restriction in LDAP.

LDAP Functional Components

In LDAP there are only two functional components: the LDAP client and the LDAP server. They communicate with each other by exchanging commands and replies. The client issues commands and the server responds with replies to those commands. LDAP allows the client and server to communicate over a TCP connection or a TLS (or SSL) connection. The previous version of LDAP specified a way to communicate over the connectionless UDP protocol. RFC 2251 defines the following commands that can be initiated by the LDAP client.

- Bind. Create a connection to the server.
- Unbind. End the connection that was created by the Bind.
- Search. Find entries in the Directory.

- Compare. Determine if a value supplied by the client is equal to a value in a specified entry in the Directory.
- Add. Create a new entry in the Directory.
- Modify. Change an entry in the Directory.
- ModifyDN. Change the name of an entry in the Directory.
- Delete. Remove an entry from the Directory.
- Abandon. Terminate the execution of a previous command that is presumably taking too long to finish. This is normally used to cancel an outstanding Search command.
- Command Extension. Allow for new commands to be defined.

Command Extensions is a mechanism in LDAP that provides for future extensibility. It allows future versions of LDAP to define new commands. It also allows for vendors of LDAP products to supply new features in a standardized manner. One example of an LDAP extension is the mass import of data. The LDAP Add command allows for the addition of only one object at a time to the directory. If the LDAP client wants to initiate the addition of several thousand entries, it would have to send a separate command for each object to be added to the Directory. This requirement to submit so many separate commands is quite onerous, as is the subsequent requirement to correlate each response that is returned with the original request in order to generate a report on the various successes and failures. So, in order to facilitate this new feature, an extension could be defined that would allow the LDAP client to execute just one command that would contain all of the entries to be added to the Directory. The LDAP client initiates all LDAP messages that represent requests. Each client request causes a response to be returned by an LDAP server. Table 3.6 shows the possible responses for the commands.

Table 3.6	*LDAP requests and corresponding responses*
LDAP Client Request	**LDAP Server Response**
BindRequest	BindResponse
UnbindRequest	
SearchRequest	SearchResultEntry, SearchResultDone, SearchResultReference
ModifyRequest	ModifyResponse
AddRequest	AddResponse
DelRequest	DelResponse
ModDNRequest	ModDNResponse
CompareRequest	CompareResponse
AbandonRequest	
ExtendedRequest	ExtendedResponse

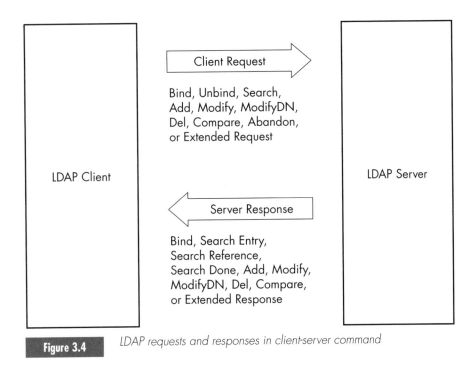

Figure 3.4 *LDAP requests and responses in client-server command*

Notice that some client requests don't require a server response, while the LDAP Search requests have more than one possible response from the server defined. Thus, the functional components have a very simple interaction, as shown in Figure 3.4.

Even though the LDAP specification defines only the two functional components, it does define the referral interaction between the client and server. With the addition of the referral concept, the functional interaction between the LDAP components can be more complex, as shown in Figure 3.5.

Thus, LDAP allows for a search that is submitted to one Directory server to be referred to some other Directory server. Notice that LDAP defines only the interaction between an LDAP client and an LDAP server. Thus the question arises of how LDAP Server 1 in Figure 3.5 knows that it is to refer a client search request to some other server, if LDAP servers don't interact. The notion that LDAP servers don't interact is a common misconception. LDAP defines only the client-server interaction but certainly does not restrict LDAP servers from using other protocols for their interaction. For example, LDAP servers can use the Common Indexing Protocol (CIP) to exchange a wide variety of information. CIP is defined in RFC 2651 and allows for the exchange of "index objects" between the participating CIP servers. When used with LDAP, each CIP index object contains selected information about the entire DIT. Both NDS and Active Directory

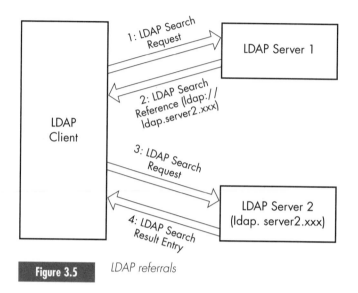

Figure 3.5   *LDAP referrals*

servers use proprietary mechanisms when they communicate to exchange update information.

Command Details

In LDAP, the LDAP client initiates all commands. If appropriate for the command, the server will reply. Note that the client may send multiple commands
to the server without waiting for a reply for each command. This mode of command is known as *asynchronous client-server communication.* This is due to
the fact that the commands and replies are not synchronized between the
client and the server. It is permissible for the client to wait for a reply to each
command prior to submitting a subsequent command. If the client is operating in this mode, then it is using what is known as *synchronous client-server
communication.*

Bind and Unbind Commands

Normally the first command that occurs in an LDAP session is the Bind. The
LDAP Bind is used to allow the client to identify itself to the server. This notion
of client identification is normally termed authentication. Depending upon the
form of the Bind, it also allows the server to authenticate itself to the client. In
LDAP version 3, there are three types of Bind commands that have been defined:

- Anonymous Bind
- Simple Bind
- SASL Bind [2]

Previous versions of LDAP defined additional Bind types, but these have been deprecated in version 3 and are no longer used. The anonymous Bind is an indication that the client either does not have an account with the LDAP server or is not willing to identify itself. If the anonymous Bind is successful, then the client will normally have limited rights on the server. It is unlikely that an LDAP server would allow an unknown server to make modifications to the DIT; thus, anonymous users normally only have access to read the Directory and cannot make changes to any entries. If the first command in an LDAP session is not a Bind, then the server should treat that command as if it had been preceded by an anonymous Bind. Thus, it would be redundant for the first command in a session to be an anonymous Bind.

The second form of the Bind is the Simple Bind. In this form, the client supplies a name and a password. If the password is omitted from the Simple Bind, then it is treated as an anonymous. Since it is considered insecure to allow the transmission of a password across the Internet, use of the Simple Bind should be allowed only over an encrypted TLS session. It might also be appropriate in situations where both the client and server are situated on the same side of a very secure firewall, and the network connections are secured from eavesdropping. All things considered, Simple Binds over TCP connections should not occur.

Note that in the simple bind, LDAP does not indicate that the octet string can contain only a static password, that is, one that is always the same from one session to another. One possible alternative to the static password is a token-based scheme, in which a token is issued to a user that displays a secret code which updates itself at periodic intervals according to some devilishly clever algorithm (known to the server). Thus, the LDAP client could include the currently displayed secret code on its token in the Simple Bind. Then the server could verify whether the code that is supplied is the one that should be displayed on the token according to the secret algorithm. If the client-supplied data agrees with the one that the server computes, then the Bind is considered successful. Note that if the Bind fails then the server will normally not close the underlying connection, and the client can try again.

The third form of the LDAP Bind is the SASL Bind. In an SASL Bind, a mechanism must be specified. The mechanism indicates the exact details of the authentication between the client and the server. The available SASL mechanisms are registered with the IANA. The most interesting SASL mechanism for LDAP is

---

2. SASL is the Simple Authentication and Security Layer and is defined in RFC 2222. SASL is a general-purpose authentication protocol that is used in a wide variety of Internet applications in addition to LDAP (e.g., POP, IMAP, and SMTP).

the "EXTERNAL" mechanism. If the SASL EXTERNAL mechanism is used, then this is an indication that the client has requested that the server use authentication information from a lower layer protocol. This lower layer protocol in the case of LDAP is likely to be TLS.

In this situation, the credentials can be omitted. If TLS authentication is used, then a successful setup of the underlying TLS connection will result in the exchange of X.509 certificate information. The part of the certificate that has been encrypted by the Certificate Authority (CA) contains attributes about the owner of the certificate that have theoretically been authenticated by the CA prior to the issuance of the certificate. The CA is the network entity that issues certificates. More details on the role of CAs and X.509 certificates will be given in Chapter 5.

Among these "authenticated attributes" is the DN of the owner of the certificate. Thus, when the SASL EXTERNAL mechanism is used, the certificates that have been exchanged at the TLS layer can be retrieved by the LDAP entities. The LDAP server can match the TLS client with some user in the Directory by retrieving the DN from the certificate and matching it with the DN of some object in the Directory. The exact set of matching rules by which an LDAP server matches the DN from an X.509 certificate with the DN of some user in the Directory is not specified by LDAP. However, it can be assumed that the LDAP server will keep a table (in some secure location) that maps the certificates that have been issued with the users that are allowed to authenticate to the LDAP server. Since there can be a mutual exchange of certificate information at the TLS layer, the LDAP client can also verify that it is talking to the correct LDAP server.

Another interesting SASL mechanism is the Digest-MD5 mechanism, which is defined in RFC 2831. Digest-MD5 authentication requires multiple exchanges of information between the LDAP client and the LDAP server. The main accomplishment of Digest-MD5 is that it allows for the authentication and verification of the user's identity without ever transmitting the password across the connection. It requires multiple exchanges of data before the security layer has been successfully negotiated. In this scenario, the LDAP client may have to issue multiple Bind commands in order to complete the negotiation successfully. Thus, Digest-MD5 can be used safely over a TCP connection with the assurance that the user's password will not be discovered. While Active Directory supports Digest-MD5 authentication, NDS does not. The use of other SASL mechanisms is possible in LDAP but will not be covered here.

Note that Bind commands may be sent at any time that an LDAP connection is open so as to modify the identity of the client. When a connection to the LDAP server is first established, the anonymous identity is used. Each subsequent Bind command that is submitted by the LDAP client changes its identity. This behavior is especially useful in situations where an LDAP client application is shared among several users. It is also useful in situations where a user has several different accounts that are used to access different LDAP services.

The companion command to the Bind is the Unbind. Whatever LDAP connection was previously established is terminated by the Unbind command. Thus, when an LDAP server receives an Unbind command, the protocol session is considered terminated. An Unbind command can also be used to abort a partially established multistage SASL Bind.

Search Command

The most used LDAP command is the Search command. This is the only standard LDAP command that is available for LDAP clients to use in the retrieval of information from the Directory. The Search command is LDAP's solution to the principal function of a Directory service (i.e., property-based information retrieval) and has the following principal parameters:

- baseObject
- scope
- derefAliases
- filter
- attributes

The baseObject field indicates where in the DIT that the server should begin its search. The search always begins at this object and possibly continues downward into the entries that it contains. The scope field indicates which of the contained entries (if any) should be used in the search. In the sample DIT shown in Figure 3.2, if the baseObject field is "O=Internet," then the different values of the scope field have the following effect on the search:

- BaseObject. Only the Directory entry "O=Internet" is included in the search.
- SingleLevel. Only the Directory entries "OU=SIDK, O=Internet," and "O=Internet" are included in the search.
- WholeSubtree. All of the Directory entries in the DIT are included in the search.

The derefAliases field describes how the client wants alias entries to be handled. An alias is a special LDAP object class, the sole purpose of which is to "point" to some other LDAP object. It has this definition:

```
( 2.5.6.1 NAME 'alias' SUP top STRUCTURAL MUST
aliasedObjectName ),
```

where the aliasedObjectName attribute is defined as

```
( 2.5.4.1 NAME 'aliasedObjectName' EQUALITY
distinguishedNameMatch
    SYNTAX 1.3.6.1.4.1.1466.115.121.1.12 SINGLE-VALUE ).
```

If a server dereferences an alias object, then when an alias is encountered in a search result, the object or entries named by the alias's aliasedObjectName attribute are substituted in the search result in place of the alias object. Dereferencing can also be carried out in locating the base object in addition to searching the subordinates of the base object. The filter field is the most important field in the searchRequest. It specifies which entries in the DIT are to be returned in the search results. The three commonly used types of filters are equality filters, substring filters, and presence filters. In an equality filter, an attribute type and an attribute value are provided. Taken together, the type and value form an Attribute Value Assertion (AVA). AVAs are used in substring filters and other filters as well. The AVA is compared against all entries in the scope of the search. The entries that match the filter are returned in the reply to the Search command. Some example AVAs are

- ObjectClass = "person"
- Cn = "bgreenblatt"
- Sn = "Greenblatt"
- O = "acme"

The substring filter type is the more complex type of filter. In the substring filter, an attribute name is given, along with the substring to match against the entries in the scope. The substring is given in the form of a wildcard string. Some example substring filters are

- ObjectClass = "*"
- Sn = "green*"
- O = "*.com"
- Description = "*finance*"

In a presence filter, only the attribute type is supplied. All entries in the scope of the Search command that have any value of the supplied attribute type are returned in the reply. The final field of the Search command is the attributes field. This field indicates which attributes from the matching entries in the DIT will be returned. A special case is used for this field when no attributes are listed. This is an indication that all available attributes from each matching entry are to be returned.

The sample DIT from Figure 3.2 will be used as the target for the example search commands. The first example will be a search to find all of the people in the Directory. There are two ways to implement this search. The best way to implement this would be to use an equality filter testing for "objectClass=person." This is better than using the presence filter with the "cn" attribute supplied. The reason that the equality filter is a better choice in this instance is that the "cn" attribute is used in several different object classes, and this filter might match entries in the Directory other than people. In this instance, "O=Internet" can be used as the base object. In many instances, an LDAP server is configured with a default search base, and the Search command can use the null string for this field. We want to search the whole subtree. This Search command has the following parameters:

- baseObject—"O = Internet"
- scope—subtree
- derefAliases—no
- filter—"objectClass = person"
- attributes—null

Now that the search has been submitted, the client will normally wait patiently for a response from the server, but it could just as well formulate another request and submit that one. LDAP does not impose any upper limit on the number of requests that a client can submit while waiting for responses to be returned. Recall the DIT shown in Figure 3.2, as the server will use it to create the response. There are five entries in the search scope (i.e., entire subtree) that match the search filter:

- Cn=breeder1, OU=SIDK, O=Internet
- Cn=breeder2, OU=SIDK, O=Internet
- Cn=breeder1, OU=french breeders, OU=SIDK, O=Internet
- Cn=louise, OU=french breeders, OU=SIDK, O=Internet
- Cn=fido's place, OU=french breeders, OU=SIDK, O=Internet

In situations where the DIT is actually spread across multiple LDAP servers, the server may return a referral. Imagine that the information shown in the sample DIT displayed in Figure 3.2 can be accessed on the LDAP server with the hostname ldap1.sidk.org. Assume that there is an additional LDAP server that is maintained by the U.S. breeders, namely, ldap.us.sidk.org. This LDAP server maintains all information in the DIT in the container, OU=US Breeders, OU=SIDK, O=Internet. Thus, the reply to the above Search command would contain a referral with an indication that the LDAP client should contact the other LDAP server. The referral is returned as an LDAP URL. The format of an LDAP URL is defined in RFC 2255. The basic format uses the string "ldap" as the protocol identifier, and the hostname is followed by the appropriate Directory context to use for a search. The LDAP URL for the U.S. Breeders OU on this second LDAP server would be

```
ldap://ldap.us.sidk.org/OU=US%20Breeders, OU=SIDK,
O=Internet
```

If the client decides that it should chase the referral by consulting the named LDAP server, then it first must create a new connection to that server. Then the client would Bind and finally perform the appropriate Search operation. This is problematic in scenarios where the LDAP client does not have appropriate credentials for the LDAP server named in the referral.

Some of the most common errors that can be returned as the reply to a Search command are

- NoSuchAttribute (16).[3] This is an indication that one of the attributes requested in the Search Request is not available for this object (or object class).
- NoSuchObject (32). This is normally an indication that the specified search base is unknown to this LDAP server.

Making Changes (Add, Modify, and Delete Commands)

LDAP defines commands that actually can change the content of the DIT. The three main commands defined are Add, Modify, and Delete. The Add command creates a new entry and places it in a specified location in the DIT. The Modify command makes changes to an existing DIT entry, while the Delete command removes an object from the DIT. Each of these commands targets only one entry. Thus, mass changes to the DIT require numerous LDAP commands.

The Add command requires the DN of the entry to be added to the DIT and a list of attribute types and values for the newly added entry as parameters. Note that the DN named in the entry field must not already exist in the DIT. Also, all mandatory attributes of the new entry's object class must also be specified. These two conditions are the most common causes for errors to be returned when using the Add command. Consider the example Add command in Table 3.7.

Table 3.7	Example Add command
Parameter	**Value**
New DN	Cn=ace breeders, OU=us breeders, OU=SIDK, O=Internet
Attributes	Cn: "ace breeders"
	ObjectClass: "top," "person," "breeder"
	Description: "World's best dogs, small and large"
	Breed: "miniature dachshund," "great dane"
	EmailAddress: "info@acebreeders.dog"

This creates a new child of the "us breeders" organization and results in the DIT in Figure 3.6.

The Modify command specifies changes to be made to an existing entry in the Directory. The Modify command requires the DN of the entry to be changed and a list to be made of changes to the entry's attributes. Each potential change is held in the "modification" field of the Modify command. This field holds a

---

3. The number in parentheses is the numeric error code assigned to this error by RFC 2251.

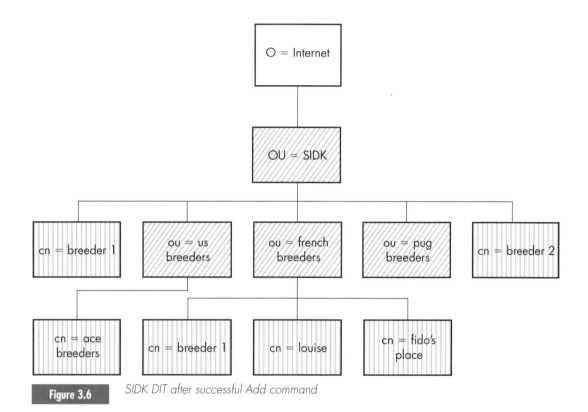

Figure 3.6   *SIDK DIT after successful Add command*

modification type, the attribute to be changed, and an optional list of values. There are three types of changes that can be made to an attribute:

- Add. Add the values given in the modification field to the indicated attribute type.
- Delete. Remove the values given in the modification field from the indicated attribute type. If no values are given in the modification field, then the entire attribute is removed from the entry.
- Replace. Remove all values of the given type from the specified DIT entry and replace them with the new values that are specified in the modification field. Just as in the case of the previous modification type, if no values are given in the modification field, then the entire attribute is removed from the entry or is ignored if the entry does not currently have an attribute of this type.

Note that the Modify command may not remove mandatory attributes from an object. So, the cn attribute could never be removed from a person object. Consider the example Modify command, which changes the email address of the entry that was just added to the DIT along with adding a telephone number (Table 3.8).

Table 3.8	Example Modify command
Parameter	**Value**
DN	Cn=ace breeders, OU=us breeders, OU=SIDK, O=Internet
Modification	Type: Replace
	Attribute: "emailAddress"
	Value: "sales@acebreeders.dog"
Modification	Type: Add
	Attribute: "telephoneNumber"
	Value: "+1-408-555-4444"

The Delete command is the final major LDAP command that makes changes to the DIT. Its syntax is simply the name of the entry in the DIT to delete. The Delete command will fail if the specified entry has children.

There are several error conditions with these commands that commonly occur:

- InsufficientAccessRights (50). This error is returned if the identity specified in the Bind does not have the necessary privileges to perform the specified change to the DIT. Not all users are allowed to make changes to entries in the DIT. In situations, users are allowed to make minor changes to their own entries, but no further changes are allowed. Other users, like the LDAP administrator, are allowed nearly unrestricted access to make changes to the DIT.
- ObjectClassViolation (65). This error is returned when a change to an entry has been attempted that would result in missing mandatory attributes. It may also be returned when an attribute for addition is specified to an entry that is not available for that object class. For example, the attempt to add a breed attribute to a person object without also adding the breeder object class would result in this error being returned, since breed is not specified as an attribute of the person object class.
- EntryAlreadyExists (68). This error is returned when an Add command specifies an entry's DN that already is present in the DIT
- NoSuchObject (32). This error is returned when a Modify or Delete command specifies an entry's DN that can't be found in the DIT.

Lesser Used Commands (Modify DN, Compare, and Abandon)

The previous sections have specified the commands that are most commonly used in LDAP. There are three additional commands that have been carried over in LDAP from X.500 and are not widely used. But, just because they aren't widely used, that doesn't mean that they don't perform functions that are considered useful in some scenarios. The Modify DN command is used to change the distinguished name of an entry in the DIT. This command is occasionally useful when an entry in the DIT needs to be moved to some other portion of the DIT. If the object were deleted and re-added to the other portion of the DIT, then any Aliases and privileges that referenced the entry would no longer apply to the newly added entry, whereas the intention of this command is to allow the renamed command to retain its previous identity. This command takes four parameters:

- Entry. The DN of the entry to be renamed.
- Newrdn. Allows the RDN of the entry to be changed. It replaces the last DN component of the entry to be renamed.
- Deleteoldrdn. Specifies whether the attribute value that was the RDN of the renamed entry remains as a value of the naming attribute. This is usually true so that the previous RDN attribute value is deleted.
- NewSuperior. Specifies the new parent of the entry to be renamed. This parameter is optional to the command and may be absent if the parent of the entry is to remain the same.

The combination of the newrdn field and the newSuperior field specifies the new name of the entry. If the newSuperior field is not present in the request message then the newrdn field replaces the last DN component of the current DIT entry. Use of the newSuperior field can cause errors to be returned. This may happen if the user attempting to perform the operation does not have appropriate access to the portion of the DIT in which the newSuperior resides. Another cause for problems arises when the location of the DN referred to by the newSuperior would cause a referral.

The deleteoldrdn parameter normally has the value TRUE, which indicates that the DN named in the entry is no longer available. Consider the example ModifyDN command that moves the "cn=breeder1" entry in the SIDK DIT (Table 3.9).

Table 3.9	*Example ModifyDN command*
Parameter	**Value**
Entry	"Cn = breeder1, ou = SIDK, o = Internet"
Newrdn	"Cn = breeder1"
Deleteoldrdn	TRUE
NewSuperior	"ou = us breeders, ou = SIDK, o = Internet"

This creates a new child of the "us breeders" organization and results in the DIT in Figure 3.7.

Notice that the "cn=ace breeders" entry is now a child of the "ou = us breeders" entry. Previously, it had been the child of the "ou = SIDK" entry.

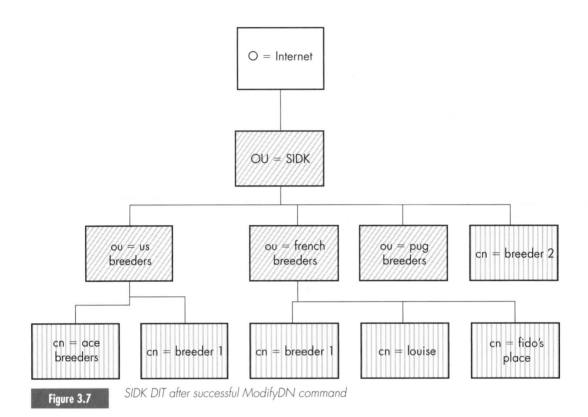

Figure 3.7   SIDK DIT after successful ModifyDN command

The Compare command allows the LDAP client to specify a single attribute type and value and have it compared to the same attribute of an existing entry in the DIT. X.500 originally defined this command to allow Directory-enabled applications to check the password that was given to them by their users with the password that was stored in the Directory. The Compare command takes the target entry and an AVA. When used in the Compare, an AVA is simply the attribute name and a potential value. The AVA field contains the attribute type and value that the server should compare to the attributes stored in the specified DIT entry. If any of the attributes of that entry have a value that is exactly equal to the specified assertionValue then the server returns true; otherwise, the server returns false.

The Abandon command is normally used in accompaniment with a Search command that seems to be taking too long. This command is useful in situations where the LDAP server is acting in tandem with other LDAP servers to perform a command. For example, a server may need to collect data from several different sources to accumulate the complete Search response, and occasionally the wait to collect the data may be very long due to the vagaries of Internet communication. Thus, the client may indicate to the server that it is unwilling to wait for completion of the command. There is no response defined or needed for the

Abandon command. The LDAP server must immediately stop working on the specified command. The Abandon command simply specifies the ID of the previous command that should be abandoned. The Abandon command is most often used when the LDAP application is operating in an asynchronous manner. In these scenarios, the immediate result of the command execution is the return of the command ID. This command ID can be used later on to retrieve the command reply or to abandon the previously executed command. In synchronous operation, the LDAP application waits until the result of the operation from the server is returned.

Extended Commands and Controls

One of the new features that is provided by LDAP version 3 versus previous versions of LDAP is the ability to define extensions to the protocol using the constructs of the protocol itself. The designers of LDAP foresaw the need to provide an extensible protocol, so that there would be no fourth version of LDAP. The extension commands allow additional commands to be defined for services not available elsewhere in LDAP. Thus an extension command would be defined for a new type of search. However, one might define an extension command to turn on and off TLS without losing the LDAP connection. Such a command would be beneficial in allowing an LDAP server listening on the same port to support both TLS sessions as well as TCP sessions. In order to define such a command, the first thing that must be defined is an OID that represents the request to start using TLS and a second OID that represents the request to stop using TLS. Since legal OIDs can start only with the digits zero, one, or two, the sample OID that will be allocated for these LDAP extended commands will start with three (which is definitely not legal). Assume that the OID 3.0 is the root of the OIDs that will be used. Thus, the OIDs for these extended commands are

- 3.0.0. Start using TLS Request.
- 3.0.1. Start using TLS Response.
- 3.0.2. Stop using TLS Request.
- 3.0.3. Stop using TLS Response.

The definitions of these new commands and replies include specification of the data that is transferred between the client and the server. Application developers are dependent upon LDAP server vendors to implement the extensions. In the case of the TLS commands, the LDAP client could include information that would aid the LDAP server in retrieving the TLS authentication information from the underlying TLS layer. Similarly, the LDAP server could include in the response field the identity that it has been assuming for the LDAP client. Given these example extended commands, the LDAP client would send this request to switch from the standard LDAP over TCP mode to the more secure LDAP over TLS mode.

Once the server has responded with a successful resultCode, the client is obligated to attempt to initiate a TLS session over the current TCP connection.

A similar client-server exchange would appear when the LDAP client was finished using TLS and wanted to return to a native mapping of LDAP onto the TCP data stream. In this case, however, the client would issue a request using the OID 3.0.2, and the server would (hopefully) respond with the OID 3.0.3. Note again that the OIDs used in these examples are completely illegal and could never be used in the construction of actual LDAP extended commands.

The other form of protocol extensions that are provided for in LDAP is the Control. LDAP Controls are additional optional parameters that can be included in any command. While the extended command is designed to provide for new kinds of requests and responses, the control is used to extend existing commands. The format of the control includes the OID that identifies the control, an indication of the criticality of the control, and the actual value of the control. The criticality field indicates what the server should do with a control that it does not recognize. If the criticality field has the Boolean value *false,* then the LDAP server can perform the command (Search or whatever) and safely ignore the control, if it does not recognize the control. If the criticality field has the Boolean value *true,* then the server *must not* perform the command and must instead return the resultCode unavailableCriticalExtension (12) if it does not recognize the control. RFC 2251 does not define any controls, but definition of several controls began immediately after the approval of LDAP version 3 as a proposed standard.

One of these controls defines an LDAP version 3-based mechanism for signing Directory commands in order to create a secure journal of changes that have been made to each Directory entry. This control is defined in RFC 2649, uses the OID = 1.2.840.113549.6.0.0, and is defined by the ASN.1 syntax

```
SignedCommand ::= CHOICE {

    SignbyServer [0] BOOLEAN

    SignatureIncluded [1] OCTET STRING }
```

This control has two choices; one is a client indication that the server should cryptographically sign the command, while the other choice allows the client to include a cryptographic signature of the command. When the client requests that the server sign the command, the server signs the data stream submitted by the client for use in creating the audit trail. This control makes use of the signature formats defined in the S/MIME specification (RFC 2311). Signed commands are presumed to be LDAP commands that modify the DIT (e.g., Add, Modify, or Delete). It allows the client to choose the criticality of the signed-Command. If it is marked critical, and the server understands the control, then the server is obligated to attach the signature included by the client to the object being modified. Thus, later on, LDAP clients can view the history of changes that have been applied to a Directory entry.

What APIs Are Available for Programming to LDAP?

The principal Application Programming Interfaces (APIs) that can be used by application developers are those that are evolutions of the original LDAP C API defined in RFC 1823. The current versions of this API are available for Java and C and are distributed as part of the Mozilla open source project at *www.mozilla.org*. These APIs are available from other sources as well. For example, the Novell Software Development Kit (SDK) includes the source for the C API. The Java 2 Enterprise Edition (J2EE) product includes the Java Naming and Directory Interface (JNDI). JNDI includes support for LDAP. Both Microsoft and Novell have designed proprietary APIs for accessing their own Directory servers. The Microsoft API, known as the Active Directory Services Interface (ADSI), also includes support for Visual Basic. The NDS API also includes support for Borland Delphi. Mozilla also has made available support for Javascript interfaces to LDAP. So, there are several mechanisms available to the application programmer to include LDAP functionality in an application. When examples are used later in the book, the Mozilla Java API will be used to provide sample code. Also, Chapter 11 will show how the Extensible Markup Language (XML) can be used with LDAP.

What Kind of LDAP Server Is Included with NDS and Active Directory?

Windows 2000 Server includes Active Directory that implements LDAP. NetWare includes Novell Directory Services (NDS), which also implements LDAP. NDS is also available on other platforms including Windows NT and many flavors of UNIX. Both NDS and Active Directory provide excellent implementations on LDAP version 3 and fully support all of the LDAP features discussed in this chapter. This includes support for all of the operations and schema definitions. More information on the details of Active Directory and NDS will be provided in Chapters 5 and 6.

Principles of LDAP Schema Design

CHAPTER OBJECTIVES

An LDAP accessible Directory may be thought of as an object store. In LDAP terminology, the stored objects are known as *entries.* The entries are arranged in a hierarchical fashion. Every entry in a Directory has exactly one parent entry and zero or more child entries. Entries with no children are termed *leaf* entries. All of the children of an entry are siblings and are said to reside in the same *container.* Each entry stores some set of information. This information is stored as a set of *attribute-value* pairs. In every entry, at least one of the attribute-value pairs is used to uniquely identify the entry among all of its siblings. For example, in a Directory storing information about people, the *email address* attribute could be used as the *naming attribute.* This scheme assumes that everyone in the Directory has an email address. Unfortunately, this is often but not always the case. For example, in a manufacturing division of a company, you typically don't find many employees with email, yet applications need to have information on these employees. Since information is hierarchical, the naming attributes of all of an entry's ancestors up the tree can be strung together to create a unique name for the entry among all entries in the Directory. This unique name is known as the entry's *distinguished name* (*dn* for short).

Not only is the LDAP data hierarchical, but the LDAP *metadata* is hierarchical as well. LDAP metadata is defined by creating *object class* and *attribute type* definitions. The entry's *object class* defines the different attributes that may be stored in an entry. An object class is defined by listing:

55

- Name. The string of characters by which the object class is known
- Mandatory attributes. Attributes that must be present in any entry of the object class
- Optional attributes. Attributes that may be present in any entry of the object class
- Superclass. The name of an object class from which this object class inherits all mandatory and optional attributes
- Type. Indicates whether objects of the type can be created in the Directory (structural) and whether the object class can be used only as a superclass in the creation of other object classes (abstract). The type also indicates whether the object class is used to augment an entry that is already stored in the Directory (auxiliary).

For example, consider the following object class definitions, taken from RFC 2256.2:

```
( 2.5.6.0 NAME 'top' ABSTRACT MUST objectClass )

( 2.5.6.6 NAME 'person' SUP top STRUCTURAL MUST ( sn $ cn )
MAY ( userPassword $ telephoneNumber $ seeAlso $
description ) )
```

In these definitions, there are two names given for each object class. The numerical *object identifier* is followed by a textual name. Then the superclass, if any, is given, which is then followed by the object class type. Finally, the mandatory and optional attributes are listed. Note that the "$" character is used as a separator. Notice that entries with the object class "person" inherit the "object-Class" attribute from the superclass. Since the "Top" object class is abstract, then no entries can be created of that class. However, entries that are of the "person" object class may be created. In the "person" object class, the "cn" attribute is short for *common name* and is normally used to give the entry the unique name within the container.

Attribute types are defined similarly. The most important parts of an attribute type are

- Name. The string of characters by which the attribute is known
- Syntax. The definition of the legal values for an attribute (e.g., character string, Boolean, etc.)
- Number of values allowed. Indicates whether there can be more than one value for the attribute in a single object class

In LDAP, most attributes are multivalued. For example, any entry with the object class "person" would have an attribute type of "objectClass" with two values:

- "top"
- "person"

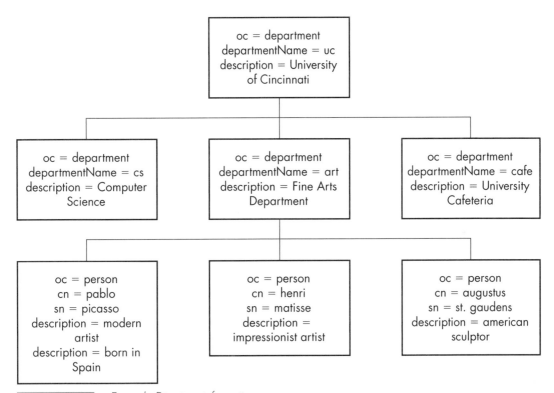

Figure 4.1   *Example Directory information*

Now, consider the following object class definition, which will be used in the creation of an example Directory tree:

```
( NAME 'department' SUP top STRUCTURAL MUST departmentName
MAY description )
```

Notice that the numerical name of the object class has been omitted for brevity. Figure 4.1 shows a pictorial view of the information in an example Directory.

In the figure, the object class names are given using the *oc* attribute type. In this example, there are seven entries, with the following dn's, with object class names given in parentheses after the dn:

- departmentName = uc (department, top)
- departmentName = cs, departmentName = uc (department, top)
- departmentName = art, departmentName = uc (department, top)
- departmentName = cafe, departmentName = uc (department, top)

- cn = pablo, departmentName = art, departmentName = uc (person, top)
- cn = henri, departmentName = art, departmentName = uc (person, top)
- cn = augustus, departmentName = art, departmentName = uc (person, top)

Note that the description attribute in the entry for "cn = pablo" has two distinct values. Information is retrieved from a Directory by using the LDAP *Search* operation. A Search operation can be used to retrieve attributes from a single entry, from entries in the container immediately below an entry, or from an entire subtree of entries. There are four parameters of interest to the Search operation (there are actually eight parameters, but the others don't affect the normalization discussion):

- Base object. The starting point for the search. This is a distinguished name.
- Scope. Indicates whether the search is for single object, container, or subtree
- Filter. Describes the conditions that must be fulfilled for an entry to be retrieved by the Search operation. The filter either matches or doesn't match an entry.
- Attributes. Gives the list of attributes that are to be returned from entries that match the filter. If an attribute is listed, then all of the values for that attribute are returned in the Search result. If no attributes are listed, then this is an indication that all attributes in the matching entries are to be returned.

Consider the following example Search operations that are applied to the sample Directory information in Figure 4.1:

- Base Object = "departmentName = uc," Scope = subtree, Filter = "description = *sculptor"
  - This search would match the one entry: cn = augustus, departmentName = art, departmentName = uc.
- Base Object = "departmentName = uc," Scope = single level, Filter = "description = *sculptor"
  - This search would not match any entries at all.
- Base Object = "departmentName = uc," Scope = subtree, Filter = "description = *artist"
  - This search would match the two entries:
    - cn = pablo, departmentName = art, departmentName = uc (person, top),
    - cn = henri, departmentName = art, departmentName = uc (person, top).

- Base Object = "departmentName = uc," Scope = subtree, Filter = "description = *"
  - This search would match every entry in the example Directory tree.

Typical Problems with LDAP Schema Design

The typical problems that can afflict an LDAP schema design are similar to those that arise in the design of a relational database schema design.[1] These problems are

- Data redundancy
- Delete anomalies
- Update anomalies
- Retrieval of unwanted data

Data redundancy occurs when the same information is repeated in many objects throughout the Directory. Collecting the information in common into a separate entry can often eliminate this data redundancy. Thus, when the common information needs to be changed, it has to be changed only in one entry, not in many entries throughout the Directory.

A delete anomaly occurs when a source object points to a target object and the target object is deleted from the Directory. This can happen frequently in Directories, since many entries have attributes that are the distinguished names of other entries in the Directory.

An update anomaly occurs when the source or target object is modified and the relationship implied by the pointer is no longer valid. Consider the situation in which an entry has an attribute that indicates a user's department number and department administrator. If the user switches departments, both of these attributes must be changed for the entry to remain valid. Similarly, whenever the department changes administrators, the entry for each user in that department must be updated with the new administrator's name.

Retrieval of unwanted data occurs when the LDAP server returns attribute values that are not needed by the LDAP client. This occurs in LDAP because the standard LDAP search operation does not allow for the retrieval of individual attribute values. In LDAP, all of the values of a particular multivalued attribute are returned to the client or none of them are. In the following sections, examples of LDAP schemas with these problems, and suggested solutions to resolve these problems, are presented.

---

1. Relational database systems and schema design are discussed in *An Introduction to Database Systems,* by C. J. Date (4th ed., Boston: Addison-Wesley, 1986).

Relational Database Normalization

In relational databases, *normalizing* the relational tables solves these problems. A relational database is made up of tables. The data types of a table are defined by the column definition. Each row in the table must conform to the definitions of the column. For example, consider a table used to represent suppliers of parts that can be ordered. In its simplest form there might just be a supplier name column and a city name column. Both of these columns are strings. In this case, the supplier name column would be considered a *primary key* since it uniquely identifies the row. This means that there can't be two rows in the table with the same supplier name.

There are many normalization rules in database theory, but the basic, most widely used are first, second, and third normal forms. These rules are summarized here:

- First normal form. A table is said to be in first normal form if all of the cells in the table contain only atomic values. This means that sets of value are not allowed in individual cells.
- Second normal form. A table is said to be in second normal form if every nonkey attribute is fully dependent on the primary key. It must also be in first normal form.
- Third normal form. A table is said to be in third normal form if all nonkey attributes are dependent only on the primary key. If a nonkey attribute is dependent on an attribute in addition to the primary key attribute, this can lead to the update anomalies mentioned above.

In moving from second normal form to third normal form an additional table (or more) is created. The typical example uses a table to hold user address information. This table would have the following five columns:

1. User Name (key)
2. Street Address
3. City
4. State
5. Zip Code

This table is in second normal form since the user name determines columns 2–5. It is not in third normal form since columns 2–4 always determine the zip code in column 5. Thus, to move to third normal form, this table must be split into two separate tables, each of which obeys the rules of third normal form above.

These three rules of normalization can be applied to LDAP schema design in order to eliminate some of the common problems. In order to apply the normalization rules to LDAP schema design, simply replace *table* in the rules with *object class,* replace *primary key* with *relative distinguished name (RDN),* and replace *cell* with *attribute value.* This gives these rules for LDAP Schema Normalization:

- First normal form. An object class is said to be in first normal form if all of the attribute values in the object class contain only atomic values. This means that sets of values are not allowed in an individual attribute value.
- Second normal form. An object class is said to be in second normal form if every nonkey attribute is fully dependent on the RDN. It must also be in first normal form.
- Third normal form. An object class is said to be in third normal form if all nonkey attributes are dependent only on the RDN. If a nonkey attribute is dependent on an attribute in addition to the RDN attribute, this can lead to the update anomalies mentioned above.

Data Redundancy

Consider the following enhanced person object class definition:

```
( NAME 'enhancedPerson' SUP person STRUCTURAL MUST ( email )
MAY ( streetAddress $ city $ state $ postalCode ) )
```

Using this schema definition, every person in the Directory would have data stored about their mailing address. In organizational directories where virtually all users have common address information, this is a tremendous waste of space and has the potential for inconsistent data. A better solution is to eliminate the redundancy by normalizing[2] the postal information into a separate object class.

```
>( NAME 'enhancedPerson' SUP person STRUCTURAL MUST ( email )
MAY postalInformationDN )

( NAME 'postalInformation' SUP top STRUCTURAL MUST ( cn $
streetAddress $ city $ state $ postalCode ) )
```

Notice that the person information only stores the name of some other object in the Directory that holds the actual information. The postalInformation object class is specifically designed to hold this information.

Figure 4.2 shows an example Directory with this information.

---

2. The term "normalizing" is used to recall the techniques of relational database schema design.

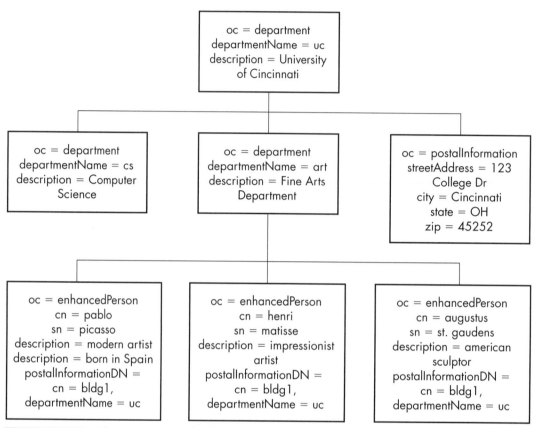

Figure 4.2 *Eliminating data redundancy*

Retrieval of Unwanted Data

In LDAP, all values of an attribute are returned in a search result if the attribute type name is listed in the *attributes* field of the search filter. This can be a problem if an entry has numerous values for an attribute and the LDAP client is really only interested in one or two of the values. Consider the scenario of secure email. In typical public-key technology implementation, if one user named Alice wants to send an encrypted message to another user named Bob, Alice must first retrieve Bob's public key.[3] When the public-key information is stored in a Directory, it is often stored in a special format, known as a *Certificate*.[4]

---

3. *Network Security: Private Communication in a Public World,* by Charlie Kaufman, Radia Perlman, and Mike Specifier (Englewood Cliffs, N.J.: Prentice Hall, 1995).
4. *RFC 2459: Internet X.509 Public Key Infrastructure, Certificate and CRL Profile,* by Russ Housley et al. (IETF, 1998).

A typical LDAP schema definition allows Bob's certificate to be stored in his Directory entry using the following object class definition:

```
( NAME 'strongAuthenticationUser SUP top AUXILIARY MAY
( userCertificate ) )

( 2.5.4.36 NAME 'userCertificate' SYNTAX
1.3.6.1.4.1.1466.115.121.1.8 )
```

Since the definition of userCertificate doesn't specify the number of values, the attribute can hold any number of values. In certain military and highly secure environments, a single user can hold many hundreds of certificates.[5] In this situation, even if the LDAP client wants only to retrieve a single certificate, all of the user's certificates are retrieved and must be examined one at a time in order to find the desired certificate. Not only are all the certificates returned by the LDAP server, they are returned unordered, so the LDAP client may have to examine each certificate in the entry to find the desired certificate. A typical certificate is about 2K bytes. Thus, the LDAP result containing 250 certificates would contain about 500K of data. Thus, in addition to the computational overhead of examining each certificate in order to find the right one, the network overhead would certainly slow down the response time. A better situation is to enhance the schema and revise the DIT. An alternate schema to solve this problem is proposed in a current Internet Draft.[6] This schema contains the following object class definition:

```
( NAME 'certificateType' SUP top STRUCTURAL MUST typeName
MAY ( serialNumber $ issuer $ validityNotBefore $
validityNotAfter $ subject $ subjectPublicKeyInfo $
certificateExtension $ otherInfo ))
```

This definition extracts many fields from the certificate data structure in order that they may be easily searchable by standard LDAP search operations. All of the fields except for certificateExtension are defined as SINGLE-VALUE. Notice that it does not include a certificate attribute. This is because the certificate is still attached to the certificateType entry using an auxiliary object class, such as strongAuthenticationUser. This new design for the DIT places all of a user's certificates in a container beneath the user's entry in the DIT rather than directly attached to the entry as in the previous design. Figure 4.3 illustrates this new DIT.

---

5. This scenario was disclosed to me in a private conversation with an individual in the U.S. Department of Defense's Defense Information Systems Agency (DISA). I don't have any more details on it, but I haven't any reason to believe that it is not a valid scenario.
6. *Internet Draft, (work in progress): LDAP Object Class for Holding Certificate Information,* by Bruce Greenblatt, published by the IETF, 2000. The latest revision has the file name: draft-greenblatt-ldap-certinfo-schema-02.

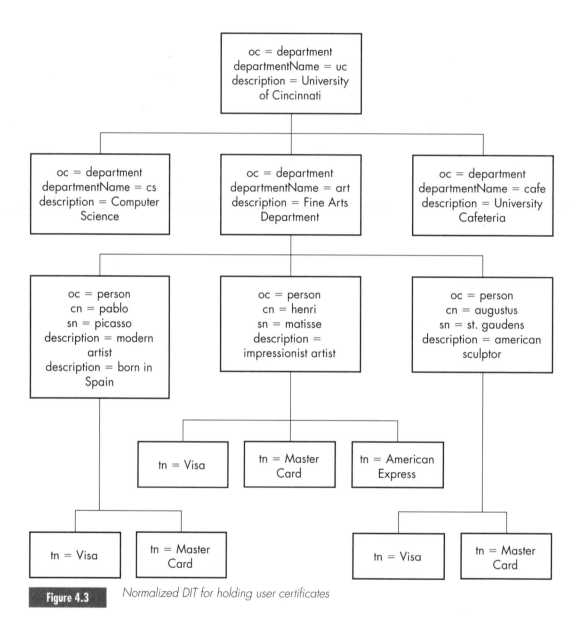

Normalized DIT for holding user certificates

In this DIT the user *henri* has three certificates, which are found in the entries immediately beneath that entry in the DIT. They have these distinguished names:

- tn = Visa, cn = henri, departmentName = art, departmentName = uc
- tn = Master Card, cn = henri, departmentName = art, departmentName = uc

- tn = American Express, cn = henri, departmentName = art, department-Name = uc

This allows an LDAP search operation to retrieve exactly the certificates that it wants and no more. For example, to retrieve henri's Visa certificate, this search could be issued:

- Base Object = "cn = henri, departmentName = art, departmentName = uc," Scope = single level, Filter = "typeName = Visa"
  - This search would match only tn = Visa, cn = henri, departmentName = art, departmentName = uc

If the alternate schema had been used, all of the certificates for the user henri would have been stored in the userCertificate attribute. The LDAP client would have to retrieve all of the certificates and parse through them to find the one that had been issued by Visa. Notice that this still allows for the easy retrieval of all of henri's certificates. This is done using the following search operation:

- Base Object = "cn = henri, departmentName = art, departmentName = uc," Scope = single level, Filter = "objectClass = certificateType"
  - This search would match all three certificateType entries in the DIT below bruceg's entry.

This same mechanism of restructuring the DIT and redefining classes can be used anywhere that attributes can have numerous values and LDAP clients need to retrieve the values only a few at a time. This mechanism also makes it simple to find all of the certificates from a single issuer or a certain type. For example, to find all of the certificates in the art department that are from Visa, the following search operation is used:

- Base Object = "departmentName = art, departmentName = uc," Scope = subtree, Filter = "typeName = Visa"
  - This would match the three Visa certificateType entries in the DIT.
    - tn = Visa, cn = henri, departmentName = art, departmentName = uc
    - tn = Visa, cn = pablo, departmentName = art, departmentName = uc
    - tn = Visa, cn = augustus, departmentName = art, departmentName = uc

In these examples, the entire certificateType entry is retrieved. Note that it is possible to just retrieve the certificate itself by naming the userCertificate attribute type in the attributes field of the Search operation. Note that if there are multiple Visa certificates for a single user, then the userCertificate attribute would have multiple values for this certificateType entry. If this situation arises, a new naming scheme for the certificateType entries should be employed.

Delete and Update Anomalies

Delete and Update Anomalies occur in LDAP when there is a reference in one entry to the distinguished name of another entry. When the referenced distinguished name is deleted or renamed, the entries references are no longer valid. Some LDAP implementations go to great pains when entries are deleted or moved to make sure that all objects that reference the modified or deleted entry are updated as appropriate.

A better solution that eliminates these anomalies is to restructure the DIT to take advantage of the hierarchy. Some object classes use the technique of placing the distinguished names of the referenced entries directly in the entry as in this standard LDAP object class:

```
(2.5.6.9 NAME 'groupOfNames' SUP top STRUCTURAL MUST
( member $ cn ) MAY ( businessCategory $ seeAlso $ owner
$ ou $ o $ description ) )
```

where the member attribute has this definition:

```
( 2.5.4.31 NAME 'member' SUP distinguishedName )
```

The use of the SUP designation in the attribute type definition is similar to its use in the object class definition. It is an indication that the syntax and matching rules in the specified SUP attribute type are to be used in this attribute type definition. Using this definition, each time a member in the groupOfNames is deleted or renamed, the groupOfNames object must be updated so that all of the member attribute values are valid. A better solution is to remove the member attribute from the groupOfNames object class and to place all member entries in the DIT beneath the groupOfNames object. Unfortunately, this is not a general solution since it does not allow the same member entry to enjoy membership in multiple groups. However, there are many applications in which restructuring the DIT in this way can be achieved.

An Example

An LDAP schema can be designed that holds the same information as a relational database schema. Using the above recommendations for the same problems can be avoided in LDAP schema designs that are avoided using normalized relational database schemas. Consider the relational database schema in Table 4.1.[7]

---

7. The schema shown in Table 4.1 is taken directly from Date's chapter on schema normalization, and forms a basis for the TPC-H benchmark defined by the *Transaction Processing Performance Council.*

Table 4.1	Sample relational database schema	
Table Name	**Column Name**	**Syntax**
Supplier	Supplier Number	Character String
Supplier	City Name*	Character String
City Status	City Name	Character String
City Status	Status	Integer
Part	Part Number	Character String
Part	Part Name	Character String
Part	Color	Character String
Part	Weight	Integer
Supplier Shipment	Supplier Number*	Character String
Supplier Shipment	Part Number*	Character String
Supplier Shipment	Quantity	Integer

This schema represents information about parts that can be ordered from various suppliers. Columns with an asterisk ("*") at the end of their names are nonkey columns that are primary keys of another table. These columns are called *foreign keys.* A company has offices in various cities and can order parts from various suppliers that have parts available. The different suppliers and their locations are represented in the *Supplier* table (Table 4.2). The status of each of the company's offices is represented in the *City Status* table (Table 4.3). Information about the different parts that can be ordered is represented in the *Part* table (Table 4.4). Finally, the current list of parts that have been ordered from various suppliers is represented in the *Supplier Shipment* table (Table 4.5). It is assumed that any part can be ordered from any supplier and that each supplier is located in only one city. This schema is already in third normal form.

Table 4.2	Data in the Supplier table
Supplier Number	**City**
S1	London
S2	Paris
S3	Paris
S4	London
S5	Athens

Table 4.3   *Data in the City Status table*

City	Status
Athens	30
London	20
Paris	10
Rome	50

Table 4.4   *Data in the Part table*

Part Number	Part Name	Color	Weight
P1	Nut	Red	12
P2	Bolt	Green	17
P3	Screw	Blue	17
P4	Screw	Red	14
P5	Cam	Blue	12
P6	Cog	Red	19

Table 4.5   *Data in the Supplier Shipment table*

Supplier Number	Part Number	Quantity
S1	P1	300
S1	P2	200
S1	P3	400
S1	P4	200
S1	P5	100
S1	P6	100
S2	P1	300
S2	P2	400
S3	P2	200
S4	P2	200
S4	P4	200
S4	P5	400

Assume that the database tables have the information in Tables 4.2 through 4.5. Now, how can we create an LDAP schema to represent this same information? It is straightforward to create an object class that has the same attributes as each table. However, it is crucial to understand the foreign key relationships, as this will help in creating the DIT structure. Whenever possible, if a table holds a foreign key then LDAP entries that are in the object class that correspond to that table should be children of LDAP entries that correspond to the table in which the foreign key is a primary key. For example, the City column of the Supplier table is a foreign key. It is the primary key in the City Status table. Thus, Supplier entries in LDAP should be children of City Status entries. This leads to the first two object class definitions:

```
( NAME 'cityStatus' SUP top STRUCTURAL MUST (cityName
$ status) )
```

```
( NAME 'supplier' SUP top STRUCTURAL MUST supplierNumber )
```

Notice that the supplier object class does not include the cityName attribute. This is because the attribute is implied by the parent-child relationship and can be retrieved from the DN of the supplier entry. Figure 4.4 illustrates the portion of the resulting DIT that is made up of entries from these two object classes.

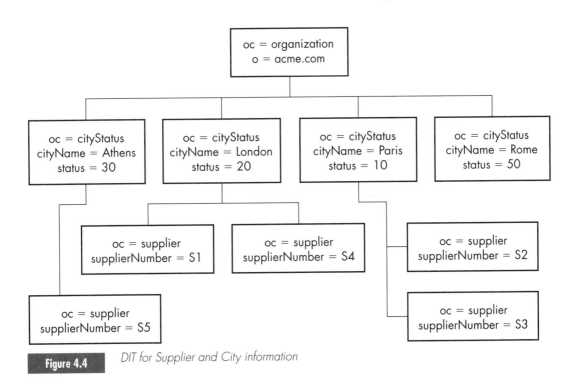

Figure 4.4   *DIT for Supplier and City information*

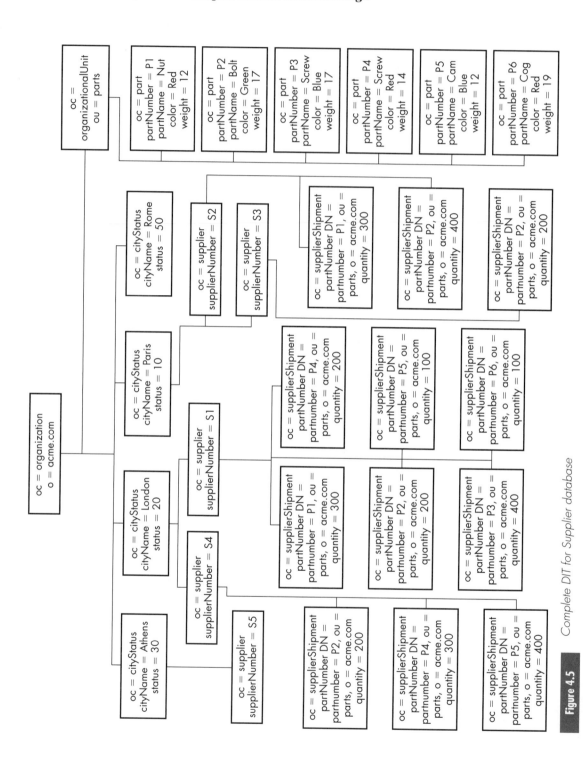

Figure 4.5   Complete DIT for Supplier database

In Figure 4.4, notice that each supplier entry is a child of the city entry in which it is located. Thus, the DNs for the supplier entries are

- supplierNumber = S1, cityName = London, o = acme.com
- supplierNumber = S2, cityName = Paris, o = acme.com
- supplierNumber = S3, cityName = Paris, o = acme.com
- supplierNumber = S4, cityName = London, o = acme.com
- supplierNumber = S5, cityName = Athens, o = acme.com

One of the properties of the relational database schema is that cities can be represented in the database, even when there are no known suppliers in that city. Notice that this representation preserves that property.

Notice too that the Part table has no foreign keys. Its entries can reside at the same level in the DIT as the City entries. But for clarity, they will all be placed in an organizationalUnit entry called *ou = parts*. Supplier Shipment entries are another matter. It has two foreign keys. One of the foreign keys is chosen as the parent entry in the DIT, while the other is used as a reference. In LDAP object classes references to other entries are always represented as DNs. This leads to the other two object class definitions:

```
( NAME 'part' SUP top STRUCTURAL MUST (partNumber $
partName $ color $ weight) )

( NAME 'supplierShipment' SUP top STRUCTURAL MUST
( partNumberDN $ quantity ) )
```

These object classes will use these attribute type definitions:

```
( NAME 'cityName' SUP name )

( NAME 'status' SYNTAX 1.3.6.1.4.1.1466.115.121.1.27 )

( NAME 'supplierNumber' SUP name )

( NAME 'partNumber' SUP name )

( NAME 'partName' SUP name )

( NAME 'color' SUP name )

( NAME 'weight' SYNTAX 1.3.6.1.4.1.1466.115.121.1.27 )

( NAME 'partNumberDN' SYNTAX 1.3.6.1.4.1.1466.115.121.1.12 )

( NAME 'quantity' SYNTAX 1.3.6.1.4.1.1466.115.121.1.27 )
```

The syntaxes used in these attribute type definitions are defined in RFC 2252. The complete DIT that corresponds to the information in the relational database defined in Tables 4.2 through 4.5 is shown in Figure 4.5.

Notice that this representation allows for only a single order from each supplier. If there is a requirement for multiple orders from a single supplier, the supplierShipment object class would have an order number attribute. As long as each order number was unique, this new attribute would allow for the creation of multiple orders from a single supplier. Since this was not a requirement in the relational database schema, it was not added as a requirement for the LDAP schema. In the DIT, each supplierShipment entry is a child of the corresponding supplier and has a pointer to the part number that was ordered from the supplier. Searching for various items in this DIT is straightforward. Consider the following problems and the resulting LDAP searches:

- Find all orders for part number P3
  - Base Object = "o = acme.com," Scope = subtree, Filter = "(&(objectClass = supplierShipment) (partnumberDN = 'partnumber=P3, ou = parts, o = acme.com'))"
- Find all orders for supplier number S2
  - Base Object = "supplierNumber = S2, cityName = Paris, o = acme .com," Scope = single-level, Filter = "objectClass = supplierShipment"

When new orders need to be entered into the system, then new supplierShipment entries need to be created in the DIT. For example, to add an order for 500 units of part number P4 from supplier number S3, the following Add operation should be initiated.

- New entry name.—"partnumberDN = 'partnumber=P4, ou = parts, o = acme.com', supplierNumber = S3, cityName = Paris, o = acme.com"
- Attributes:
  - ObjectClass—Top, supplierShipment
  - Quantity—500

Notice that the DN of the part number is used as part of the DN of the supplierShipment entry. While this makes for long DNs, it is not illegal. However, for convenience in the real world, order numbers would probably be used as discussed above.

Summary

As shown in this chapter, the rules of SQL normalization can be directly applied to the hierarchical nature of LDAP schema and DIT designs. Thus, output from any number of data modeling techniques can be used to represent the LDAP schema and DIT structure. The chapter shows how the lessons learned in SQL database normalization can be applied to LDAP by eliminating data redundancy, reducing the possibilities of unwanted data retrieval, and showing how delete and update anomalies can be eliminated in certain circumstances.

LDAP Security

CHAPTER OBJECTIVES

There are three aspects to security as it applies to LDAP. The first aspect is traditional network security. Since LDAP is a client-server protocol, sensitive data is often transmitted across the network between the client and the server. The second aspect of LDAP Security is Access Control. LDAP Access Control defines the means by which an LDAP server determines which users have the ability to read and write to specified entries in the Directory. The third aspect of LDAP Security relates to authentication. Authentication refers to the techniques by which the LDAP server confirms the identity of the user that is attempting to gain access via the LDAP client. Both NDS and Active Directory provide excellent features that implement all three aspects of LDAP Security. While there are currently standardized mechanisms in place for network security and authentication, there are currently no standardized mechanisms for LDAP access control. Both NDS and Active Directory have implemented similar, proprietary access control mechanisms.

Network Security

Network security provides safeguards against various threats that may be targeted against computer networks. As Directories are a network application service, they could be prime targets for these threats. Typical attacks against a Directory involve the theft of information that is stored in the Directory and the denial of service to a Directory client. If a rogue user gains access to the Directory, then that user may be able to change the Directory information and cause the Directory to provide incorrect answers to the clients' queries.

In order to provide a complete Directory service, some level of network security must be provided. But, what parts of security are relevant to Directories? Users need to prove who they are since some data that the Directory stores is marked with access control information indicating who is allowed to read and write it. Some systems prove users identities by trusting the IP address from which the request comes or by sending a password across the network. Neither of these techniques is secure. A better way is through cryptography, which provides knowledge of a secret without divulging it. Using cryptographic techniques allows a Directory client to prove to the Directory server that it knows the password without ever sending the password across the network. Thus, even if there is an eavesdropper on the connection between the client and the server, the user's password is still safe.

Authentication is the process of determining whether someone or something is, in fact, who or what it is declared to be. It is often the case that a Directory client must be authenticated to the Directory server before being granted access to the Directory information. Secure forms of authentication involve the process that provides knowledge of a secret without divulging it. There are two types of secrets. In the first type, both sides (i.e., the client and the server) know the same secret. In the other type, known as public-key schemes, each user has a pair of keys, one public and one private, which are mathematically related such that you can verify that someone knows the private key by using the public key. Authentication is the primary use of security in Directory systems.

Various security mechanisms that Directories use are introduced here. A complete discussion of network applications can be found in Kaufman, Perlman, and Speciner's book *Network Security: Private Communication in a Public World.* The most basic tool used in network security is *encryption.* Encryption allows data to be modified into a form that allows it to be hidden from unauthorized people. The encrypted form of the data is known as the cipher data. Decryption is the process that these authorized people use to transform the cipher data back into the original data. Authorized people encrypt and decrypt data by making use of keys that are used by the encryption or decryption process. A key is a short piece of data that is known only to the authorized people. Keeping the key secret allows the encryption algorithms to be published. The typical use of encryption in Directories is to keep certain data private as it is transferred across the network between the Directory client and server. There are a large number of encryption algorithms that can be used to provide this privacy, and the most widely used ones fall into two categories:

- Public-key algorithms use a pair of keys that are created in a special process that allows one key to be used in encryption and the other key to be used in decryption. One of the keys is kept secret (the private key), and the other key is made widely available (the public key).

- Secret-key algorithms use only a single key that is used for both encryption and decryption.

Items to note about these two types of encryption algorithms are

- Public-key algorithms are substantially slower than secret-key algorithms. In fact, public-key algorithms are so much slower that they are rarely used for encrypting data that is larger than a few kilobytes.
- The keys used in public-key algorithms are much larger than the keys used in secret-key algorithms. The key used in the popular RSA public-key algorithm defined in RFC 2437 is normally 256 bytes to provide adequate security. The key used in the popular RC5 secret-key algorithm defined in RFC 2040 normally uses only 8 or 16 bytes.
- Great care must be taken in transmitting the key used in the secret-key algorithm among the authorized users. If any unauthorized users gain access to the key, then any data encrypted using that key has been compromised.

Secret-Key Encryption

The most common secret-key encryption algorithms operate on a fixed length segment of data at a time, usually 8 or 16 bytes. The algorithms take this data segment in combination with the secret key as input data in order to produce the encrypted data. The encrypted data is almost always the same size as the input, plain text data. When the data to be encrypted is longer than the segment that the algorithm is designed to accept, the plain text data is broken into several blocks which are encrypted one at a time. For example, if a document to be encrypted is 100 bytes long, and the encryption algorithm operates on data blocks that are 8 bytes long, then the document would be divided into 13 blocks. Note that the last block of data would not be 8 full bytes, but only 4 bytes long. In order to decrypt the data, the algorithm uses the encrypted data along with the same secret key that was used in the encryption.

Some algorithms are defined to encrypt each block independent of all the other blocks of data. Alternatively, the algorithm can use the results of a previous block in the input to the encryption of the next block. The details of any particular encryption algorithm are beyond the scope of this book. However, it can be assumed that if a document has been encrypted with a strong secret-key encryption algorithm, then the encrypted data may be safely transmitted across the Internet. As long as only the originator and the intended recipient know the key used in the encryption process, any malicious intruders that may intercept the document cannot decrypt the document.

Public-Key Encryption

In public-key encryption algorithms, two keys are required. One key is used in the encryption process, and another key is used in the decryption process.

In public-key technology, the two keys must have some sort of special relationship to each other and are generated by a special mathematical process at the same time. Each pair of keys belongs to a user. The user will publish one of the keys (i.e., the public key) in order to make it available to other users. The other key (i.e., the private key) is kept confidential and is not made available to anyone else. For example, if Alice wants to send Bob a secret message, she would retrieve Bob's public key (perhaps from a known Directory) and use it to encrypt the message. Once the message has been encrypted, only Bob can decrypt it using his private key. Thus, even though Alice knows the public key, the plain text data, and the encrypted data, she still cannot derive Bob's private key. This is due to the special mathematical relationship between the two keys. In one popular encryption algorithm, the attempt to derive the private key would require the potential attacker to factor a large number. This large number is in the range of the size of the key. If the key is 1,024 bits, then the attacker would have to factor a number in the range of $2^{1,024}$ power, which is a number with more than a 100 decimal digits and, therefore, nearly impossible to guess or derive.

Public keys should be widely published. If Alice published her public key so that it is widely available, anybody who needs to send her encrypted data can easily retrieve Alice's key and securely send her information. Even though you can and should widely publish public keys, you need to know the mapping from name to key. A good way of providing this mapping is by storing Alice's public key in a Directory that provides this mapping for the user. A Directory client can provide Alice's email address, and the Directory server will be able to perform the lookup to find the entry in the Directory that contains Alice's public key and return it to the end user. The preferred way that public keys are published in the Directory is by making use of the certificate format defined in the X.509 Recommendation of the ITU. The strongAuthenticationUser auxiliary object class is defined in RFC 2256 for this purpose. A user's certificate is stored in the userCertificate attribute. This object class is defined as

```
( 2.5.6.15 NAME 'strongAuthenticationUser' SUP top
AUXILIARY

MUST userCertificate )
```

Thus, userCertificates can be attached to any entry in the Directory. When a user's certificate is needed, that user's entry in the Directory is found, and the user's userCertificate attribute is retrieved via LDAP. Because early versions of LDAP defined a special version of the certificate format, when certificates are retrieved the binary specifier must be used with storing and retrieving this attribute. Thus, when retrieving it, *userCertificate;binary* is used so that all of the ASN.1 encoding defined in X.509 is preserved. A CA issues a certificate, and then it is stored in the Directory. Currently, versions of NetWare and Windows 2000 Server include a CA that allows for the creation of certificates and their storage in Active Directory and NDS (as appropriate). Other companies supply CA products that are able to store certificates in LDAP as well.

Message Digests, Digital Signatures, and Authentication

Another security algorithm of special interest is the message digest algorithm. A message digest algorithm takes any size document as input (i.e., the message) and produces a fixed-size data block as output. This fixed-size data block is called the *message digest*. For example, the popular MD5 message digest algorithm is described in RFC 1321: *The MD5 Message Digest Algorithm*. MD5 produces a 16-byte message digest of its input. The message digest is also called a fingerprint because of the analogy to a person's fingerprint. Just as it is extremely difficult to find two people with the same fingerprint, it is also extremely difficult to find two documents that produce the same MD5 message digest. A good message digest algorithm has the property that it is computationally infeasible to produce two messages having the same message digest. Similarly, it is also computationally infeasible to produce any message having a given prespecified target message digest.

A message digest algorithm must have these properties to be useful in the creation of digital signatures. If Alice wants to create a digital signature for a document, first she must create the message digest of the plain text document. Then Alice will encrypt the message digest using her private key. Alice can then send the plain text document along with the document's signature to Bob. Bob can verify the digital signature by first creating the message digest of the plain text document. Then Bob will decrypt the digital signature using Alice's public key. If the decrypted digital signature and the message digest that Bob created are identical, then Bob has *verified* Alice's signature. In verifying the digital signature Bob is guaranteed of two facts:

- The document that Bob received is precisely the document that Alice sent, and it has not been altered en route.
- The document was actually sent by Alice and no other person. This is due to the fact that no other person could have created the digital signature since it required the use of Alice's private key, and only Alice has access to her private key.

Digital signatures are especially useful in directories for the purpose of authentication. The digital signature process can be used in this scenario. Once the client connects to the server, the server provides the client with a piece of data that the client must sign. Once the server verifies the signed data, the server is assured of the identity of the client, and the client can continue operating on the Directory.

TLS

TLS is explained in RFC 2246 and defines a mechanism for the creation of a secured connection across the network. TLS directly makes use of the services provided by TCP. Internet applications, such as Web Browsers, connect to

Internet servers, such as Web servers, by creating a connection known as a *socket* between the application and the server. A socket can be viewed as a pipeline between the application and the server through which data may be exchanged once it is created.

TLS provides the primary mechanism by which LDAP connections can be secured. TLS provides means for encrypting and digitally signing the data that is transferred between the client and the server. LDAP clients and servers are not directly involved in encrypting and signing the data. It is handled by the underlying connection between them. Furthermore, TLS provides a useful means of providing authentication when used with the SASL authentication mechanism.

The creation of a socket is very analogous to the dialing of a telephone call. Once the telephone number is entered, the destination line rings. When the receiving party answers the ringing telephone on his or her end, a telephone connection is established. In order to create a socket connection between two entities on the Internet, the calling party (known as the client) enters an Internet address. A program running on the client's machine attempts to make a connection to a program. If there is any program listening for connections on the server's machine then the connection can be established. All of the Internet transports that are used in LDAP make use of sockets for communication between clients and servers but use different types of sockets. The sockets for all of the transport types have similar behavior. Thus, when they are used for the simple transport of data between the client and the server, the different socket types can be used by the Directory entities in virtually the same way.

During the attempt to create a socket, the client and server go through the same handshaking described in Chapter 2. During the TLS handshaking process, the client and server each exchange some information before the socket can be created. If either side is not satisfied with the information that is provided by the other side (known as its peer) then the attempt to create the socket is broken off, and no socket connection is created. A very simplified view of the handshaking that occurs in the TLS layer was shown in Figure 2.2.

In this view of the handshaking that occurs during the attempt by a TLS client to open a socket with a TLS server, both the client and the server send two pieces of information across the network prior to a successful TLS socket creation. The client initiates the handshaking when it sends a special message defined by TLS, known as a *client hello*. This message contains various parameters that define those kinds of TLS services that are being requested. For example, the TLS client can request that the connection be encrypted by any of several different means. It can also request that any data being passed across the socket is to be compressed. The client hello message also includes some randomly generated data that aids in the creation of the encrypted connection. The server responds to a client hello with another special message that is defined by TLS, known as a *server hello*. The main piece of information included in the server hello message is information that is unique to the server, known as a certificate. The server presents its certificate in such a way that the client can verify that it really does belong to the server. This verification is known as *au-*

thentication. The precise details of how this authentication works are not particularly important to the functions of Internet Directories, but a short overview of the authentication process is given later in this chapter. The important feature of this first stage in the handshaking process is that it has allowed the TLS client to verify that the TLS server to which it has connected is indeed the one that it intended to contact.

Once the client has authenticated the server, the second phase of the TLS handshaking can begin. The objectives of the second phase are to allow the server to authenticate the client and to create an encryption key that allows all data passed across the TLS session to be kept confidential. If the server requested client authentication in its server hello message, then the client is obligated to provide its certificate information in the subsequent message. At this time the client uses the random data that it provided in the client hello message along with information that is in the server certificate to generate the encryption key. Simultaneously, the server is performing the same process, thus guaranteeing that the client and server have generated the same key, often known as a *shared secret.* If the server is satisfied with the client certificate information that the client has provided, then it provides a response that indicates that the connection has been opened successfully. Keep in mind that this explanation of TLS connection creation has been greatly simplified and, while accurate, many details have been omitted.

As far as LDAP application programmers are concerned, once the connection to the server is set up, all LDAP operations proceed in an identical manner regardless of the underlying socket type. Thus, in scenarios where sensitive data is to be carried across the network, then a TLS connection should definitely be used. Since TLS also provides for the digital signing of the data carried across it, even when sensitive data is not carried, TLS provides useful services even when its data encryption service is not needed or used. By having the data digitally signed, the primary benefit is the prevention of data corruption. Even though there is a performance penalty in the creation of the TLS socket versus the creation of the TCP socket, in many instances the additional features of TLS make it worth paying that cost. Since virtually no code in the LDAP application is changed when a TLS socket is used in place of a TCP socket, the application programmer needs to consider the type of data that is transmitted when determining whether or not to enable the use of TLS. Whenever possible, both options should be presented to the administrator of the deployed application, and the administrator should be allowed to configure the application to use TLS or TCP.

Access Control

There are two aspects to LDAP access control. The first aspect is the traditional mechanisms by which an LDAP server determines whether or not an authenticated user has permission to perform the various LDAP operations. If a user attempts to perform an operation on an LDAP entry that it is not authorized to perform, the LDAP server will return the error InsufficientAccessRights (50). This error is returned if the identity specified in the Bind does not have the necessary privileges to perform the specified change to the DIT. Not all users are allowed to make changes to entries in the DIT. In most situations, users are allowed to make minor changes to their own entries, but no further changes are allowed. Other users, like the LDAP administrator, are allowed nearly unrestricted access to make changes to the DIT.

Unfortunately, LDAP has not yet provided definitions for standardized access control. The primary model currently under consideration allows only for the assignment of rights to DIT entries that pertain to their access and manipulation using Directory operations. This model is based upon the access control models defined in NDS and Active Directory. Both of these models are similar. The NDS model and terminology will be used in the following presentation. However, nearly identical features exist in Active Directory. Note that if the LDAP application is required to manipulate the access control information in the DIT, it must make use of proprietary APIs provided by NDS or Active Directory. Thus, the application must provide separate libraries, if it needs to work with both of these popular implementations. Following the discussion of NDS specific access control, platform independent mechanisms will be discussed.

Native NDS Access Control

Consider the DIT of a typical NDS installation in Figure 5.1. Notice that it includes several entries that are useful in administering a network. In NDS it is typical to group users and the resources that they use in the same containers. This allows for easy creation of access control rights for the users and those resources. In addition to the user's login script attribute mentioned above, there are other attributes in the user object class that allow for the control of how and from which locations in the network the user may log in, and what resources that user may use. Every entry in NDS contains an *Access Control List* (ACL) attribute that has been added to the top object class. In NDS, the ACL is the key component in determining Directory access control. The ACL determines which operations a trustee entry can do on another entry and its attributes. In the schema, the ACL is a multivalued attribute type assigned as an optional attribute to the object class Top.[1] Because all object classes inherit the characteristics of Top, all entries could have an ACL attribute. Since it is an optional attribute in Top, not all entries in NDS will have an ACL. In NDS, the ACL has three fields:

- Protected Attribute Name
- Subject Name
- Privileges

---

1. The original implementation did not support auxiliary object classes. Instead, it added attributes to the standard object class, such as adding the ACL attribute to the Top object class.

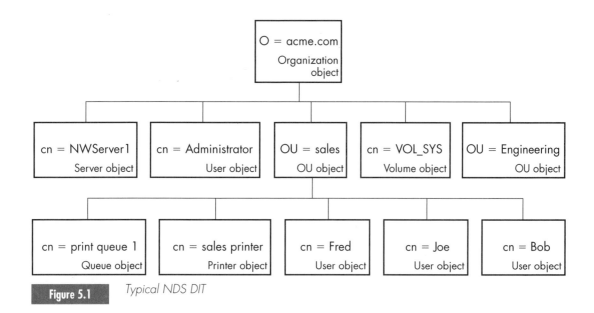

Typical NDS DIT

An ACL value can protect either an object or an attribute. The protected object is always the one that contains the ACL attribute. If an ACL entry is to apply to the object as a whole, the protected attribute name is empty. If a specific attribute is to be protected, it is named in the ACL entry. Note that even though the ACL can contain only one attribute name, since the ACL can be multivalued, a separate ACL can be included for each attribute that is to be protected. The Privileges field is a bit mask representing the kind of access being granted (value 1) or denied (value 0). The interpretation depends on how the bits are used, as shown in Table 5.1.

Table 5.1	*NDS ACL Privileges interpretation*	
Bit Mask	**Individual Attributes**	**Entry Rights**
0x00000001	Compare Attributes	Browse Entry
0x00000002	Read Attribute	Add Entry
0x00000004	Write, Add, Delete Attributes	Delete Entry
0x00000008	Add/Delete Self	Rename Entry
0x00000010	(none)	Supervisory
0x00000020	Supervisory	(none)

Since the Privileges value of the ACL is a bit mask, two bit-mask values are combined if the rights are to be granted. For example, to grant browse, creation, and deletion rights to an entry, the three bit-mask values are added together to create a Privileges value of 0x00000007. The ACL is interpreted in a slightly different manner depending on whether an individual attribute is being protected or whether the entry as a whole is being protected. The Add Entry right (i.e., bit-mask value 0x00000002) gives the user identified in the Subject Name field of the ACL the right to create entries in the DIT beneath the object to which the ACL is attached. If this same bit-mask value mentions an attribute type name in the Protected Attribute Name field, then the user identified in the Subject Name field is given the right to read the attribute in question.

Normally, the Subject Name field in an ACL contains a distinguished name. However, NDS has defined several special values that have special significance. The two most useful values that can be used here are

- [Root]. Denotes the Directory tree root object.
- [Public]. Includes all object in the tree.

Thus, if an ACL contains the value "[Public]" in the Subject Name field, then that is an indication that all users in the tree have been granted the privilege mentioned in the ACL. Not only does NDS allow for individual entries to be used in the Subject Name field, it also allows for containers to be used. Remember that the ACL is an attribute on the object that is being accessed. The ACL attribute lists the trustees and the rights they have to the object. For example, if object Joe in Figure 5.1 had Browse [Entry Rights] over OU=Engineering, the ACL on the object OU=Engineering would look like Table 5.2.

Table 5.2   *Sample NDS ACL*

ACL Field	Value
Subject Name (Trustee Name)	CN=Joe, OU=sales, O=acme.com
Protected Attribute ID	[Entry Rights] (Rights apply to the whole entry, not just an attribute.)
Privilege Set	Browse

Now, consider an ACL on the *CN=sales printer* object in Figure 5.1 that allows every one to print. This ACL, which is attached as an attribute to the printer object, would be as in Table 5.3.

Table 5.3   *Sample NDS ACL to allow access to the Sales printer*

ACL Field	Value
Subject Name (Trustee Name)	OU=sales, O=acme.com
Protected Attribute ID	[Entry Rights] (Rights apply to the whole entry, not just an attribute.)
Privilege Set	Browse, Add

This ACL works because access rights in NDS are inherited. All users in a container inherit the rights that have been assigned to the container. So, in this instance, Joe and Fred now have rights to use the Sales printer. Not only do Joe and Fred have these rights, but also, whenever a new user is added to the OU= Sales container, that new user will automatically inherit these rights as well. NDS allows administrators to control how rights are inherited. A special kind of ACL called an Inherited Rights Filter (IRF) specifies which rights can be inherited from an object to entries below it in the Directory. The IRF (sometimes called an inheritance mask) takes the place of the trustee name in the ACL ([Inherited Rights Filter] appears in the Trustee ID field). It can be applied to [Entry Rights], [All Attributes Rights], or specific attribute rights. Consider the ACLs that are applied to the NDS tree in Figure 5.2 after the user Bob as been added in the organizational unit called Engineering (see Table 5.4).

Table 5.4	Sample NDS ACLs			
ACL Number	**Object Holding ACL**	**Trustee**	**Protected Attribute**	**Privilege Set**
1	O=acme.com	Sales	[Entry Rights]	Browse + Delete
2	OU=Engineering	Fred	[Entry Rights]	Create
3	Bob	Joe	[Entry Rights]	Delete

If no object in the Directory has an IRF, Joe would have the following effective rights:

- The Delete right to Fred because Fred's ACL grants this right to Joe in ACL Number 3
- The Delete right to acme.com and OU=engineering, O=acme.com because sales is part of Joe's Distinguished Name (this makes Joe security equivalent to Sales). Two NDS objects are said to be *security equivalent* when granting a right to one of the objects also automatically grants that right to the other object. In this case, granting the rights to OU=sales automatically grants those rights to all of the objects in the sales container because of the way NDS objects inherit rights.
- The Browse right to Bob, Engineering, and acme.com because Joe is security equivalent to Sales.

Notice that even though Joe has been named as the trustee in only one of the ACLs above, through NDS's notions of ACL inheritance and security equivalence, he has been granted additional rights. In the definition of the User object class there is an attribute called securityEquals. This multivalued attribute lists all of the other entries in NDS that are security equivalent to this user. If Joe's securityEquals attribute lists Fred, then Joe will also have the following right granted in the ACLs in Table 5.4:

- The Create right to Engineering and Bob because Joe is Security equivalent to Fred.

Now, suppose that OU=Engineering has an IRF that masks the *Delete* right. This ACL looks like Table 5.5.

Table 5.5	Sample IRF		
Object Holding ACL	**Trustee**	**Protected Attribute**	**Privilege Set**
OU=Engineering	[Inherited Rights Filter]	[Entry Rights]	Delete

This means that if Joe had been granted Delete rights to the O=acme.com container then that right would be filtered out for all objects in the OU=Engineering container. In order to calculate the access rights that any NDS object A has to any other NDS object B, the following rights are taken into account:

- Rights specifically granted to A
- Rights granted to all containers (all the way back to the root container) that A is in. These are *inherited* rights.
- Rights granted to any object to which A is security equivalent, including any rights that these security equivalent objects inherit
- Rights that have been filtered out to A and any objects to which it is security equivalent
- Rights that have been granted to the special NDS object [Public]

Fortunately, NDS always calculates these rights, and they never need to be calculated by the NDS user. NDS has a command *NWDSGetEffectiveRights* that allows the NDS user to retrieve the rights that any NDS object has to any other NDS object. Furthermore, whenever a user A attempts to access an object B, NDS calculates A's rights to B before allowing the access. NDS uses this mechanism to control access to printers, files that are stored in the NetWare file system, and many other network resources. So, network administrators can control access to any network resource that is represented in NDS.

Another important feature of NDS access control is that whatever rights are granted to a group entry in the DIT are inherited by all the members of the group. This works the same way in which rights granted to a container in the DIT are inherited by all of the entries in that container. So, even when groups contain other groups, the inheritance passes on, no matter how deeply the groups are nested. Furthermore, the assignment of rights to groups and containers works together. Thus, if an organizationalUnit entry is a member of a group, then any assignment of rights to the group passes along to all entries in the subtree underneath the organizationalUnit entry. Similarly, if a Group entry is underneath some organizationalUnit container, then all members of the group inherit any assignment of rights to the organizationalUnit. Again, it is important to remember that even though it uses different terminology, Active Directory provides a very similar implementation of access control and is not missing any necessary features.

Application-Defined Permissions

While NDS and Active Directory provide excellent mechanisms for protecting the entries in the DIT, they do not directly support the kinds of access control required by many applications, so those applications have to implement their own permissions management. Consider an electronic commerce application. This application provides various items that can be purchased by visitors to a Web site. Different users within an organization have the authority to create and modify the items that are available for purchase. There are also different properties of the item, such as

- Price
- Shipping Weight
- Description
- Number in Inventory

It is desirable to require special rights to change the price of an item or to have the ability to reorder an item from a supplier. The people who have these rights may not be the same people who have the rights to simply make changes to the item's description. While it may not be particularly useful to keep the properties of the item in an entry in the DIT, LDAP provides features that make it very useful to store access control information for the item in the DIT. However, it is not appropriate to use the NDS or Active Directory access control mechanisms defined above for this. Just because a user has the rights to modify an entry or subtree in the DIT doesn't mean that user should be allowed to change the price of an item. Similarly, just because a user (possibly a network administrator) has modify rights to the subtree in which the electronic commerce information is stored does not necessarily mean that the organization wants to grant the administrator rights to change the price of an item for sale on the organization's Web site.

Since the system-defined access control mechanisms of NDS and Active Directory are not generally useful for implementing application-defined permissions, alternative mechanisms are required. Fortunately, both LDAP implementations have enhanced the default behavior of the Group object class. The enhancement is provided through a *groupMembership* attribute. Whenever an entry is added as a value to the member attribute of a Group, that same Group is added as a value in the entry's groupMembership attribute. The groupMembership attribute has behavior similar to the securityEquals attribute. An entry does not have to be specifically listed as a value in the Group's Member attribute for the Group to show up as a value in the entry's groupMembership attribute.

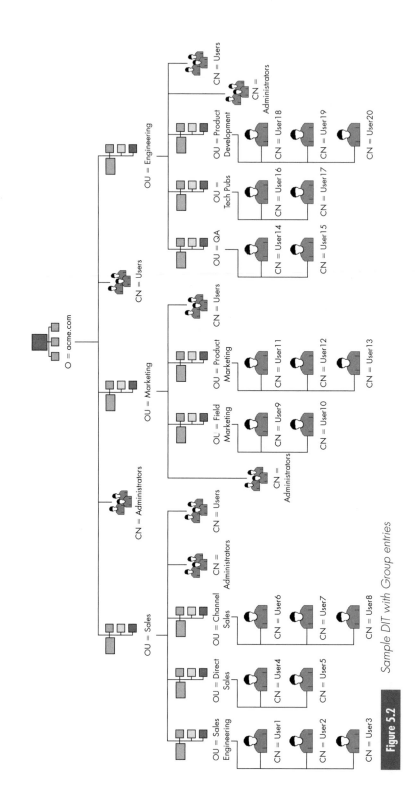

Figure 5.2

Sample DIT with Group entries

The groupMembership attribute behaves similarly to NDS's securityEquals attribute. Whenever a container is added as a value to a Group's member attribute, that Group is added as a value to the groupMembership attribute of all entries in the subtree underneath the container. Additionally, all the members of the group inherit the groupMembership attribute values. Even when groups contain other groups, the inheritance passes on, no matter how deeply the groups are nested.

Consider the DIT in Figure 5.2 that illustrates various Groups and Users in the organizational hierarchy. The DIT has the following Group entries and their member attribute values:

- cn = users, ou = engineering, o = acme.com
  - cn = user16, ou=tech pubs, ou = engineering, o = acme.com
  - ou = qa, ou = engineering, o = acme.com
  - cn = user18, ou = product development, ou = engineering, o = acme.com
- cn = administrators, ou = engineering, o = acme.com
  - cn = user15, ou=qa, ou = engineering, o = acme.com
  - cn = user19, ou = product development, ou = engineering, o = acme.com
- cn = users, ou = marketing, o = acme.com
  - cn = user9, ou=field marketing, ou = marketing, o = acme.com
  - cn = user11, ou = product marketing, ou = marketing, o = acme.com
  - cn = user12, ou = product marketing, ou = marketing, o = acme.com
- cn = administrators, ou = marketing, o = acme.com
  - cn = user10, ou=field marketing, ou = marketing, o = acme.com
  - cn = user13, ou = product marketing, ou = engineering, o = acme.com
- cn = users, ou = sales, o = acme.com
  - cn = user6, ou = channel sales, ou = sales, o = acme.com
  - cn = user7, ou = channel sales, ou = sales, o = acme.com
  - cn = user4, ou = direct sales, ou = sales, o = acme.com
  - ou = sales engineering, ou = sales, o = acme.com
- cn = administrators, ou = engineering, o = acme.com
  - cn = user8, ou = channel sales, ou = sales, o = acme.com
  - cn = user5, ou = direct sales, ou = sales, o = acme.com
- cn = users, o = acme.com
  - cn = users, ou = engineering, o = acme.com
  - cn = users, ou = marketing, o = acme.com
  - cn = users, ou = sales, o = acme.com
- cn = administrators, o = acme.com
  - cn = administrators, ou = engineering, o = acme.com
  - cn = administrators, ou = marketing, o = acme.com
  - cn = administrators, ou = sales, o = acme.com

Notice that the Groups have Users, organizationalUnits, as well as other Groups as members. Based upon the above list, here are a few example entries and the values in their groupMembership attribute:

- cn = user8, ou = channel sales, ou = sales, o = acme.com
  - cn = administrators, ou = engineering, o = acme.com
  - cn = administrators, o = acme.com
- cn = user15, ou=qa, ou = engineering, o = acme.com
  - cn = users, ou = engineering, o = acme.com
  - cn = administrators, ou = engineering, o = acme.com
  - cn = administrators, o = acme.com

The operational behavior of the groupMembership attribute can be leveraged in our implementation of application-defined permissions. We can create groups that represent the permissions that are defined by the application. For example, in the previously mentioned electronic commerce application, we can define two Groups. The member attribute of the first Group would hold the list of entries that have permission to change the price of the item. The member attribute of the second group would hold the list of entries that have permission to reorder items from a supplier. Thus, in order to determine if a user has the permission to perform an action that is represented by a Group, the application needs only to check if that Group is a value in the user's groupMembership attribute. This checking is best done using the LDAP Compare operation. This works, even if the permission has not been directly granted to the user due to the way that the inheritance of the groupMembership attribute works. Care must be taken when using this mechanism. If privileges are granted on a user-by-user basis, and the Groups end up with enormous numbers of values (millions?) in their member attributes, several problems can arise. First, there can be an extreme performance penalty in the server's computation of the groupMembership attribute values. Second, since LDAP does not provide a way to selectively retrieve values of an attribute, if the member attribute ever needs to be retrieved, then there is a substantial memory and performance overhead. Third, just by their very nature, attributes with large numbers of values are difficult for administrators to deal with. Thus, whenever possible the values of a Group's member attribute should be containers in the DIT or other Group entries.

Authentication

One of the most important aspects of the administration of the Directory Service is the control of how information that is stored in the Directory is made available to various requesters and how the Directory identifies the requester of the data. This identification is often termed *user authentication* or just *authentication*. LDAP servers authenticate the user by means of a Bind operation.

While this section does not pretend to present a complete list of all of the possible means of authenticating users to Directory services, the most commonly discussed means are presented. Various authentication means that have been defined for Directory services are as follows:

- Anonymous authentication
- User ID and Password in the clear, also known as *simple authentication*
- User ID and Password across an encrypted TLS link, often called *protected authentication*
- Challenge Response mechanisms
- Exchange of X.509 credentials, known as *strong authentication*
- Authentication via TLS
- Authentication via SASL
- Authentication as defined in X.509

In anonymous authentication, the Bind operation does not contain any information that can be used to identify the requesting user. Typically, all anonymous users are given identical access to Directory information. In simple authentication, the Bind operation contains the name of the user and a sequence of bytes that is only known by the named user. This sequence of bytes is known as the *password*. If this password matches the password stored by the Directory Service then the Bind operation is presumed to be successful, and the connecting user is given access to the Directory information according to the access granted to that user.

In protected authentication, the Directory server is "listening" on a TLS port in accordance to the definitions of TLS as defined in RFC 2246. Proposals have been made for a *Start TLS* extended operation that would allow for TLS and TCP connections to be made to the same server port, but this mechanism has not yet been standardized. For example, LDAP version 3 defines that the default port to listen on for incoming TLS connections is 636. Once the TLS client and TLS server finish their negotiation, both the LDAP client and the LDAP server have exchanged a session key that is used to secure the communications across the TLS connection. The session is secured because all data that is passed over the connection is encrypted using the negotiated key. Thus, the entire Bind operation that contains the user name and password is encrypted for protection as that information travels across the Internet.

An interesting alternative to the submission of the user's password across the LDAP connection is the use of the challenge response mechanism. One example of such a mechanism is defined in RFC 2195. This mechanism is known as CRAM-MD5, which stands for Challenge Response Authentication Mechanism-MD5.[2] MD5 is the secure message digest algorithm defined in RFC 1321. MD5

---

2. A somewhat stronger SASL mechanism, known as DIGEST-MD5, is also available and is preferred by Active Directory as an authentication choice. DIGEST-MD5 is defined in RFC 2831.

has the special property that it produces 16 bytes of output data from arbitrary input data. By using CRAM-MD5 as an authentication method, the LDAP client is allowed to bind to the LDAP server without sending the password across the network. A challenge response mechanism works in the client-server paradigm as follows:

1. The client contacts the server in order to authenticate.

2. The server responds with some string of bytes, possibly including a randomly generated byte sequence. This string of bytes is known as the "challenge."

3. The client combines its password with the server's challenge in a special way that is defined by the Challenge response mechanism and sends this combination back to the server. This combination is known as the response.

4. The server examines the response to determine if it confirms that the responding client knows the password of the user that is attempting the authentication.

In addition to allowing the client to authenticate itself to the server, some challenge response mechanisms allow the server to authenticate itself to the client. The server authentication normally takes place before the client authentication that is described above. The above challenge response mechanism allows for only a single challenge before the password-derived response is generated. Some challenge response mechanisms allow for multiple challenges to be exchanged before the password-derived response is created. In the single challenge response mechanisms, if for some reason the client contacts a "rogue" server, it may be possible for the client's password to be discovered. This is due to the fact that the rogue server may use the client's response as part of a "dictionary" attack. In this scenario, the rogue server will use a list of possible passwords and generate responses for each possibility in the list until it finds one that matches the response provided by the client. For this reason, single-challenge response mechanisms may be inappropriate when authenticating across the Internet but would be a very reasonable choice when authenticating within the corporate intranet. Note that the challenge response mechanisms never distribute the client's password, so they have attractive characteristics when compared to the simple and protected authentication mechanisms.

CRAM-MD5 is a single challenge response mechanism. The data encoded in the server's challenge contains a presumptively arbitrary string of random digits, a time stamp, and the fully qualified primary host name of the server. The syntax of the unencoded form must correspond to that of an RFC 822 "msg-id" as described in RFC 1939 (which defines POP3). The client makes note of the data and then responds with a string consisting of the user name, a space, and a "digest." The latter is computed by applying the keyed MD5 algorithm from RFC 2104. In keyed MD5 the key is a shared secret and the digested text is the time stamp (including angle brackets). This shared secret (i.e., the password) is a string known only to the client and server. The "digest" parameter itself is a 16-octet value that is sent in hexadecimal format, using lower case ASCII characters. When the server receives this client response, it verifies the digest provided. If the digest is correct, the server should consider the client authenticated, and it responds appropriately. An example from RFC 2195 using the IMAP protocol is shown below. The base64 encoding of the challenges and responses is part of the IMAP4 AUTHENTICATE command, not part of the CRAM specification itself.

```
S: * OK IMAP4 Server

C: A0001 AUTHENTICATE CRAM-MD5

S: + PDE4OTYuNjk3MTcwOTUyQHBvc3RvZmZpY2UucmVzdG9uLm1jaS5uZ
   XQ+

C: dGlt1GI5MTNhNjAyYzdlZGE3YTQ5NWI0ZTZlNzMzNGQzODkw

S: A0001 OK CRAM authentication successful
```

In this example, the shared secret is the string "tanstaaftanstaaf." Hence, the keyed MD5 digest is produced by calculating

```
MD5((tanstaaftanstaaf XOR opad),

MD5((tanstaaftanstaaf XOR ipad),

  <1896.697170952@postoffice.reston.mci.net>))
```

where ipad and opad are as defined in the keyed-MD5 RFC. When using TLS for protected authentication, an important side effect that results from its use is the ability of the LDAP client to gain access to the LDAP server's certificate. The LDAP client can then use this certificate in order to validate that it is "talking" to the appropriate LDAP server. This verification is performed by validating the authenticity of the server certificate against its set of known CA certificates. The LDAP server's certificate will have been digitally signed by one of these CA certificates. If the LDAP client is able to verify the signature on the LDAP server's certificate by using the public key from the appropriate CA, then the client can be assured that the LDAP server is authentic. The LDAP client should periodically check the Directory entries of its cached CAs in order to retrieve the CRLs. This allows the LDAP client to determine if the LDAP server's certificate is still in effect or whether it has been revoked.

The currently accepted format of certificates that is used in Directory authentication is that defined as X.509 version 3 certificates. Note that whether simple authentication or protected authentication is used, the name that is transmitted to the Directory is normally the complete distinguished name of the entry corresponding to that user (e.g., cn=bruceg, o=prentice hall, c=us).

Strong authentication provides the most powerful means of authentication between Directory clients and Directory servers. One of the most important aspects of strong authentication that distinguishes it from the other authentication means is that the user's name and password never cross the network, even in encrypted form. As in the protected form defined above, the Directory client has the ability to authenticate the Directory server. But, in the strong authentication technique, the certificate of the Directory Client is transmitted to the Directory Server, along with proof that the Directory Client knows about the private key that corresponds to the public key contained in the user certificate information. Typically, the private key is locked in the Directory client by means of a password that must be entered by the end user in order to unlock the private key for use in the strong authentication. Note that the private key never leaves the client workstation. Once the Directory Server receives the client Certificate, information in the certificate is used to authenticate the client to the Directory. One common place in the Certificate to put the user identity is in the Certificate subject-name field, but the user identity can be placed in other fields as well (e.g., the other-names Extension field). The forms of strong authentication available in LDAP are placed inside of the SASL authentication choice on the Bind operation. Here are some available strong authentication choices using SASL:

- The mechanism defined in the TLS specification mentioned above can be used.
- The strong authentication technique defined in the X.509 recommendation can be placed inside of SASL.
- Kerberos authentication can be placed inside of SASL as well (it doesn't use X.509 certificates though). Kerberos is a secure method for network authentication. It is based on secret-key authentication and in many respects is similar to the TLS handshaking process. Kerberos is not used in NDS but is used in Active Directory.

Whichever of these techniques is used, the high-level view of the exchange of X.509 certificates between Directory Client and Directory Server is the same. Directory Servers may or may not support all of these defined authentication techniques. Furthermore, Directory Servers normally give administrators the capability to turn off weaker authentication means in order to protect the integrity of the Directory information.

PART TWO

Using an Installation of Active Directory

CHAPTER OBJECTIVES

Starting with the release of the ADS component of Windows 2000, Microsoft has made available an LDAP server that is an integrated feature of the network operating system. An installation of ADS does more than just provide a generic LDAP server. It is the focal point for the administration of a Windows 2000 network. ADS provides access to every resource in the network. It allows the administrator to manage relationships between users and the network devices, network applications, and other information in the network. This chapter is intended to provide only a brief overview of some of the important features of ADS as they relate to LDAP developers. For a more comprehensive look at ADS, the reader should consult an ADS reference. Several fine books provide detailed information on ADS.[1]

The most important aspect of ADS for our purposes is its excellent implementation of LDAP. This chapter will discuss what types of objects are normally created in the DIT, how basic access to those objects is controlled, and finally how the directories replicate the information in the DIT across the network from one Directory server to another. This chapter will also discuss several advanced features of ADS that are not normally considered part of the basic definition of LDAP.

---

1. See *Windows 2000 Active Directory,* by Alistair G. Lowe-Norris (Sebastopol, Calif.: O'Reilly, 2000), and *Creating Active Directory Infrastructure,* by Curt Simmons (Upper Saddle River, N.J.: Prentice Hall, 2000).

Because ADS is an excellent implementation of LDAP, in most scenarios LDAP developers do not have to write any special code to make sure that their applications will work with ADS. Even installation programs that modify the base schema of ADS do not have to be written specifically for ADS. More details about schema modifications will be given in Chapter 9. The main area that application developers may want to investigate that is specific to ADS is its implementation of Access Control. LDAP has not defined any standard mechanism for deciding which users can access which LDAP entries. Thus, each LDAP server vendor implements access control features in a different way. Thus, if it is necessary for an LDAP application to manipulate access control information, the application must include modules that are built specifically for each supported LDAP server. Just to compound matters, there is not a foolproof way using LDAP to determine whether the LDAP server that is being used is actually ADS.

It is also important to note that Microsoft has defined several new object classes that are specifically designed to hold information about Users and other entities that are important for the successful administration of a Windows 2000 network (e.g., Computers, Shares). Finally, ADS servers that are cooperating to provide the network Directory service use a proprietary mechanism so that changes made to entries at one LDAP server are automatically replicated to other servers throughout the Windows 2000 network. This allows for LDAP applications to be replicated throughout the network and not be dependent on a single ADS server instance. The LDAP applications can be installed at various sites throughout the network, and the installation at each site can use an ADS server instance installed at that site. If the LDAP application makes changes to an entry locally, it can be assured that those changes will be replicated to all ADS server instances that hold duplicates of that entry in its data store.

A Typical ADS Installation

Our investigation of ADS will cover what happens during installation, some aspects of the Directory schema that are peculiar to ADS, and how data is replicated across the network. Even though you can assume that ADS is already installed when an LDAP-enabled application is to be deployed, it is still useful to understand the process of installing and configuring ADS. This is because ADS will be the principal infrastructure upon which the LDAP applications that we develop will rely. Similarly, even though the data replication behavior of ADS is transparent to the LDAP applications, the fact that the ADS can easily replicate the LDAP data across the network makes it possible for our LDAP applications to be painlessly distributed across the network.

Consider what happens when a Windows administrator first installs ADS. ADS is installed when an administrator creates the first Windows 2000 server in the network. When that server is installed, ADS is installed as well. The server on which ADS is installed is called a *Domain Controller.* Several objects are created in the Directory that are representative of real objects that need to be administered. The principal objects that are created upon ADS initialization are

- A user entry that represents the administrator of the network
- A computer entry that represents the domain controller for the Windows 2000 server that was just installed
- Various default groups for managing security relationships in Windows 2000
- A domain context container into which the above objects are placed

The object classes for these entries are not standard LDAP object classes. Instead, Microsoft has defined new object classes that are subclasses of the standard object classes. For example, consider the User object class that is defined by ADS. Note that this has the same name as an NDS object class, but it is very different and can be distinguished as such by the unique Object Identifier that Microsoft has assigned for it. Recall that each LDAP object class has two names: the string representation and the OID representation:

```
( 1.2.840.113556.1.5.9 NAME 'user' SUP top STRUCTURAL
MUST (governsID $ defaultObjectCategory $ defaultSecurity
Descriptor $ rDNAttID $ lDAPDisplayName $ schemaIDGUID $
subClassOf $ systemAuxiliaryClass $ systemMayContain $
objectClassCategory $ systemPossSuperiors $ systemOnly) MAY
(accountExpires $ lastLogon $ lastLogoff $ networkAddress
$ scriptPath $ userCertificate $ . . . )²
```

Notice that Microsoft's definition of the User object class is a subclass of Top, whereas Novell's definition of the User object class is a subclass of the X.500/LDAP OrganizationalPerson. It is also interesting to note that Microsoft has also taken the liberty of augmenting the Top object class with numerous additional attributes not defined as part of the LDAP schema specified in RFC 2256.

While Novell uses the X.500 style Organization and OrganizationalUnit as the primary containers in the DIT, Microsoft has decided to use the domain-Context as the primary container for structuring the DIT. This approach (known as *dc-naming*) is based on the definitions of RFC 2247. Dc-naming allows a natural progression from the Windows NT 4.0 Directory model in which most objects are stored in a single domain. In NT 4.0, users, printers, and so on, are organized into *domains.* When a user logs in to a domain, depending upon the privileges the user has been granted, access is given to the printers and shared file systems in that domain. Each domain has one or more servers that are assigned as *domain controllers.* There is no hierarchy in the domain. All objects are stored at the top level. If an enterprise has more than one domain in their

---

2. The ADS schema actually defines numerous other attributes for the User Object Class, but they have been omitted here for brevity.

network, then the administrator may configure the domain controllers to share user authentication information. This allows a user to log in to one domain, and access printers in another domain. Since the top-level containers in ADS will be domainContext objects, LDAP applications must allow for them to be used. For example, consider an application that stores a default search base. For this application to work with ADS, the application must allow for this configuration parameter to be configured using dc-naming principles.

Each ADS domainContext is analogous to a single Windows NT domain. This mapping allows for easy migration of data from the domain system to ADS. Because Microsoft also stores DNS information in the DIT, each domainContext also maps to a single Internet domain name. It is not clear that either of the NDS or ADS naming approaches is any better than the other one (especially since NDS stores DNS information without using dc-naming). They are just different ways of approaching the same problem. So, upon installation, a typical ADS DIT appears as in Figure 6.1.

ADS is the central repository for all Windows 2000 administrative information. There is much more to Windows 2000 than just the network Directory, but ADS is the mechanism that allows the administrator to control the other features of these modern operating systems. The initial DIT of ADS actually contains several more objects than are shown above. Notice that the Computers container is initially empty. This is due to the fact that when ADS is first installed, the only computer in the network will be the domain controller on which ADS is located. This computer is placed in the Domain Controllers container instead. Notice also that there is no object in the DIT comparable to the Volume object

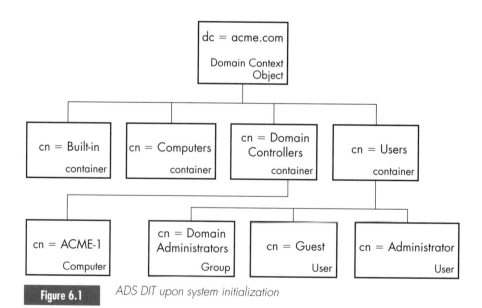

Figure 6.1   *ADS DIT upon system initialization*

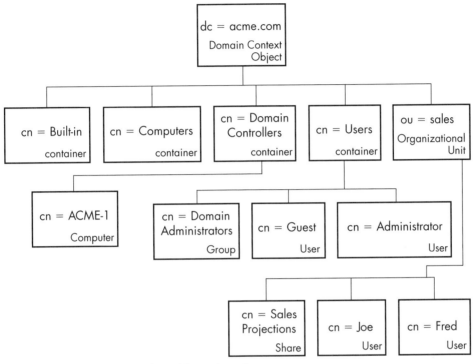

Figure 6.2   *ADS DIT after adding a few objects*

in the NDS initial DIT. This is because in ADS, the administrator must decide which shared volumes get published into the ADS DIT.

As more users, printers, and other objects get added to the ADS DIT, the top-level organization would get more crowded, so it should get subdivided into organizational units as well. So, after a few entries are added to ADS, the DIT might appear as in Figure 6.2.

Notice that the ADS administrator has added a new organizational unit to the tree for the sales organization within acme.com. Two new users, a printer, and an associated print queue have also been added to this new organizational unit container. It is appropriate in ADS to group users and the resources that they use in the same containers. This allows for easy creation of access control rights for the users and those resources. Every object in ADS contains a *Security Descriptor* that has been added to the top object class. This Security Descriptor contains the entry's *Discretionary Access Control List*. In ADS, the DACL is the key component in determining Directory access control. The DACL contains a list of *Access Control Entries* (ACEs) and determines which operations a user entry can perform on another entry and its attributes. In the schema, the ACL is a single-valued attribute type assigned as an attribute to the object class *Top*.

Because all object classes inherit the characteristics of Top, all entries will have an ACL attribute. In ADS, the ACE has five fields (see Table 6.1).

Table 6.1	ADS ACE fields
ADS ACE Field	**NDS ACL Analog**
AccessMask	Privileges
AceType	Protected attribute name
Trustee	Subject name
AceFlags	N/A
Flags, ObjectType, InheritedObjectType	Protected attribute name

An ACE value can protect either an object or an attribute. The protected object is always the one that contains the ACE attribute. The Flags subfield determines whether an ACE entry applies to the object as a whole. The Flags subfield has the following possible values:

- Neither
- Both
- ObjectType only
- InheritedObjectType only

The *Neither* and *Both* values refer to whether the ObjectType or InheritedObjectType subfields apply. If the ACE applies to the object as a whole, then Flags is Neither, while ObjectType or InheritedObjectType are both NULL. If a specific attribute is to be protected, then Flags is ObjectType only, and the ObjectType subfield contains the attribute to be protected. The ObjectType subfield does not actually contain the name of the attribute that is protected by the ACE. Instead, it contains a special identifier called a Globally Unique Identifier (GUID). In ADS, a GUID is a 16-byte value that is assigned to every object in the DIT upon creation. This GUID is kept in the object's *objectGUID* attribute. ADS has added the objectGUID attribute to the Top object class. In this case the GUID refers to a schemaIDGUID that is held in the schema object, which ADS holds in the DIT. This schemaIDGUID defines the attribute in the ADS schema. Note that even though the ACE can only contain one attribute name, since the DACL can have many ACEs, a separate ACE can be included for each attribute that is to be protected. The ObjectType and InheritedObjectType subfields store GUIDs that indicate what the ACE actually applies to.

ADS allows the ACE to apply to child objects as well by using the AceFlags field. This field indicates whether the ACE will apply to child objects or not. Additionally, ADS will set the AceFlags to indicate whether the ACE has been inherited. If the AceFlags field indicates that the ACE should apply to child objects, then assigning the Both value or the InheritedObjectType value to the Flags sub-field will finish the job. It appears that the NDS approach with multivalued ACL attributes is a slightly cleaner approach and easier to administer, but the ADS approach seems viable as well.

Since there is no standardized mechanism for access control, when using ADS, LDAP applications must use its native access control mechanisms if manipulation of Directory-based access control information is a requirement. In most situations LDAP applications do not need to manipulate the ACEs, since the ACE controls only the visibility of entries within ADS and which LDAP operations can be used against which entries. If an LDAP application stores user configuration information in ADS, there is no need to create additional ACEs for any user configuration entries that are stored in LDAP. This is due to the fact that the ADS administrator will have already created sufficient access control policies that are represented by ACEs. These ACEs will sufficiently restrict access to the configuration entries, just as they do to the user entries. Thus, if a user's application configuration information is stored using an auxiliary object class, and the configuration information for an ADS user is attached to the appropriate ADS user object, then the existing ACEs that control access to the user will also control access to the user configuration information.

ADS Replication

ADS allows Directory data to be replicated across the network between the Directory servers. ADS divides the servers in a network into Sites. ADS performs replication more frequently among servers within a site than to servers in other sites. Thus, if servers A and B are in the same Site and server C is in another Site, then server A replicates data more frequently to server B than it does to server C. ADS replications are made to domain controllers in each site. However, a site does not actually determine what data is replicated and how the data is partitioned. The ADS domain is the unit of replication. If only part of the information in a domain context's subtree should be replicated, the domain context must be subdivided into multiple subordinate domain contexts. Consider the example in Figure 6.3.

In this example, there are eight separate domains that are defined in the ADS DIT. Each one has its own domain controller and may have many containers, users, and other objects inside of the domain. As entries are modified within each domain, they are replicated across the various sites. Since a server may hold information for multiple domains, this organization of the data has similar flexibility to the NDS Partition replication scheme. Note that since the data is replicated across multiple servers, collisions may occur in ADS just as they were described for NDS. Each ADS domain controller (there may be more than one for each domain) has a read-write copy of the DIT for that domain. Only domain

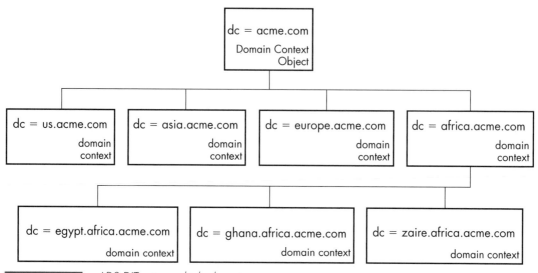

Figure 6.3   *ADS DIT using multiple domains*

controllers in a domain have writable replicas of the DIT for that domain. Domain controllers may have replicas of the DIT for other domains, but those replicas are read-only. In this scenario, domain controllers within a domain are the "masters" of the domain data. Domain controllers outside of that domain are considered slaves. Updates flow from the masters to the slaves. Since ADS allows for more than one domain controller for a domain, the replication technique that it uses is called *Multimaster Replication.*

LDAP applications can make use of the domain context information stored in ADS to do some level of self-configuration. By doing a container-level search of the root for domainContext objects, the LDAP application can easily discover the available top-level domain for the organization in which the application is installed. The domainContext information can be useful in terms of licensing. A single installation of an LDAP application could "bind" itself to a single domainContext upon registration. In other words, when the application's customer registers use of the application to the application vendor, the vendor will tie the registration code to a particular domainContext entry. If a subsequent registration of the same registration code uses a different domainContext, this registration would fail, since it would be obvious that two different customers are using the same license. If the same customer has more than one domain name, then this licensing scheme can still be used. There is only a requirement to bind each application license to a valid domain name. Since the domain contexts in ADS are tied into the DNS domain names, it is reasonable to assume that the domain contexts are as unique as the domain names in DNS.

Using an Installation of Novell's NDS

CHAPTER OBJECTIVES

Using its NDS, Novell has made available an LDAP-style Directory in its NetWare operating system since the 1992 release of version 4 of its NetWare operating system. LDAP support was added to NDS in 1997 with the availability of the LDAP Services for an NDS component offered as an add-on to versions of NDS already in the marketplace. Subsequent versions of NDS have offered the LDAP component as an integrated feature. This chapter is intended to serve as a brief overview of the NDS version of an LDAP server and to introduce the reader to some of the major features that it provides. Several fine books provide detailed information on NDS.[1]

NDS does more than just provide a generic LDAP server. It is the focal point for the administration of the network in which it is installed. Historically, this was only for NetWare based networks, but Novell has expanded the focus of NDS to allow for it to be used in the successful administration of non-NetWare networks, such as Windows and UNIX. NDS makes a list of and provides access to every resource in the network. It allows the administrator to manage relationships between users and the network devices, network applications, and other information in the network. Both Microsoft and Novell will tell you that

---

1. See Chris Andrew et al., *Novell's NDS Developer Guide* (San Jose, Calif.: Novell Press, 1999), and Jeffrey Hughes and Blair Thomas, *NDS for NT* (Foster City, Calif.: IDG Books, 1998).

their respective offering is substantially superior to its competition. While both offer many advanced features, for the typical user there are far more similarities than differences.

The most important aspects of NDS that distinguish it from a generic LDAP server are those that revolve around the ongoing administration of the network. Thus, this chapter will discuss what types of objects are normally created in the DIT, how basic access to those objects is controlled, and finally how the Directories replicate the information in the DIT across the network from one Directory server to another.

NDS also provides an excellent implementation of LDAP, and in most scenarios LDAP developers do not have to write any special code to make sure that their applications will work with NDS. Even installation programs that modify the base schema of NDS do not have to be written specifically for NDS. More details about schema modifications will be given in Chapter 9. Just as with ADS, the main area specific to NDS that application developers may want to investigate is its implementation of Access Control. Novell provides many applications that directly leverage NDS. A typical example is Novell's proxy server application known as Border Manager. Most of these NDS-enabled applications enhance the base schema in some way.

It is also important to note that Novell has long used object classes that are specifically designed to hold information about Users and other entities that are important for the successful administration of a NetWare network (e.g., Printers, Volumes). Finally, NDS servers that are cooperating to provide the network Directory service use a proprietary mechanism so that changes to entries that are made at one LDAP server are automatically replicated to other servers throughout the network. This allows for LDAP applications to be replicated throughout the network and not be dependent on a single NDS server instance. The LDAP applications can be installed at various sites throughout the network, and the installation at each site can use an ADS server instance installed at that site. If the LDAP application makes changes to an entry locally, it can be assured that those changes will be replicated to all NDS server instances that hold duplicates of that entry in its data store.

Note that the manner in which NDS handles replication is very different from the way in which ADS handles replication, as described in the previous chapter. However, it is unlikely that the LDAP developer needs to worry much about how the LDAP server goes about its business of replicating Directory entries across the network. All that is important to know is that any changes that are made to the DIT or schema in either ADS or NDS will be sent to the other ADS or NDS servers in the network. Since each LDAP server handles replication differently, ADS and NDS will not be able to replicate to each other. Normally networks will be either an all-NDS network or an all-ADS network.

A Typical NDS Installation

Consider what happens when a NetWare administrator first installs NDS. NDS is installed when an administrator creates the first NetWare version 4 or later server in the network.[2] When the first NetWare server is installed, NDS is installed as well. Additionally, several objects are created in the Directory at that time and are representative of real objects that need to be administered. The principal objects that are created upon NDS initialization are

- A user entry that represents the administrator of the network
- A server entry that represents the NetWare server that was installed
- A volume object for each volume that is created on the NetWare server. In NetWare, each server must have at least one volume on which files are stored. The server may have additional volumes. Each volume is represented by its own entry in NDS.
- An Organization container into which the above objects are placed

The object classes for these entries are not standard LDAP object classes. Instead, Novell has defined new object classes that are subclasses of the standard object classes. For example, consider the User object class that is defined by NDS. The User object class is defined as subclass of the LDAP organizationalPerson object class, which is in turn defined as a subclass of the person object class. Recall that the person object class is defined as

```
( 2.5.6.6 NAME 'person' SUP top STRUCTURAL MUST ( sn $ cn )

  MAY ( userPassword $ telephoneNumber $ seeAlso $
  description ) )
```

The organizationalPerson object class is defined in RFC 2256 as

```
( 2.5.6.7 NAME 'organizationalPerson' SUP person STRUCTURAL

  MAY ( title $ x121Address $ registeredAddress $
  destinationIndicator $ preferredDeliveryMethod $
  telexNumber $ teletexTerminalIdentifier $
  telephoneNumber $ internationaliSDNNumber $
  facsimileTelephoneNumber $ street $ postOfficeBox $
  postalCode $ postalAddress $ physicalDeliveryOfficeName $
  ou $ st $ l ) )
```

Finally, NDS defines the User object class as:[3]

---

2. NDS is also installable as a feature on other operating systems, not just as an integral feature of the NetWare operating system.

3. In NDS's definition, both attribute names and object class names can have spaces. The spaces have been removed in this presentation for compatibility with LDAP requirements.

```
( NAME 'user' SUP organizationalPerson STRUCTURAL

   MAY (accountBalance $ allowUnlimitedCredit $
   groupMembership $ higherPrivileges $ homeDirectory $
   language $ lastLoginTime $ lockedByIntruder $
   loginAllowedTimeMap $ loginDisabled $
   loginExpirationTime $ loginGraceLimit $
   loginGraceRemaining $ loginIntruderAddress $
   loginIntruderAttempts $ loginIntruderResetTime $
   loginMaximumSimultaneous $ loginScript $ loginTime $
   messageServer $ minimumAccountBalance $ networkAddress $
   networkAddressRestriction $ passwordAllowChange $
   passwordExpirationInterval $ passwordExpirationTime $
   passwordMinimumLength $ passwordRequired $
   passwordUniqueRequired $ passwordUsed $
   printJobConfiguration $ printerControl $ privateKey $
   profile $ profileMembership $ publicKey $ securityEquals $
   securityFlags $ serverHolds $ typeCreatorMap $ uID )
```

Notice how many additional attributes NDS includes in the definition of the user object class. NDS uses these additional attributes to administer users. As an example, consider the *loginScript* attribute. Whenever a NetWare user connects to the network, a series of commands is executed for the user in order to set up the user's environment appropriately. For example, various NetWare volumes can be mapped as local drives for the user's convenience. This series of commands is called the "login script." This attribute contains the login script for users. NDS also allows a loginScript attribute for organization and organizationalUnit containers. At the container level, this script is executed in addition to the user's login script. When a user logs in, NetWare's LOGIN program searches one level above (to either the Organization or Organizational Unit) and runs the container login script, before the user's login script (if any). Because NDS replicates information across each server in which the user entry is stored, the same login script will be executed by NDS no matter where in the network a user logs in.

Immediately after creation of an NDS tree and the installation of a NetWare server (both of which normally occur at the same time), a typical DIT appears as in Figure 7.1.

As more users, printers, and other objects get added to NDS, the top-level organization would get more crowded, so it is normally subdivided into organizational units. So, after a few entries are added to NDS, the DIT might appear as in Figure 7.2.

Notice that the NDS administrator has added a new organizational unit to the tree for the sales organization within acme.com. Two new users, a printer, and an associated print queue have also been added to this new organizational unit container. Thus, there are now nine objects in the NDS DIT (see Table 7.1).

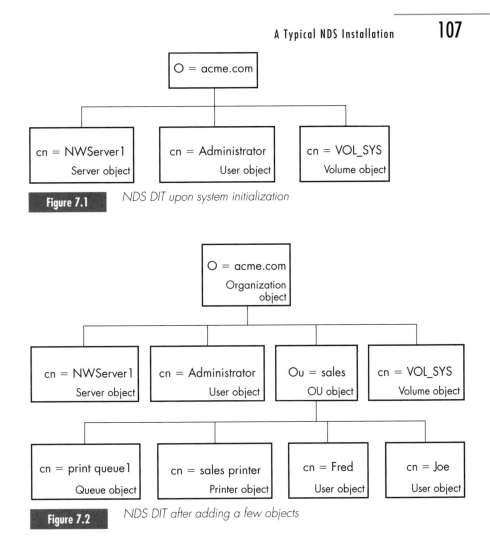

Figure 7.1   NDS DIT upon system initialization

Figure 7.2   NDS DIT after adding a few objects

Table 7.1   Objects and object classes in a typical NDS DIT

NDS Name	NDS Object Class
O=acme.com	Organization
Cn=NWServer, o=acme.com	NCP Server
Cn=admin, o=acme.com	User
Ou=sales, o=acme.com	OrganizationalUnit
Cn=VOL_SYS, o=acme.com	Volume
Cn=PrintQueue1, ou=sales, o=acme.com	Queue
Cn=SalesPrinter, ou=sales, o=acme.com	Printer
Cn=Fred, ou=sales, o=acme.com	User
Cn=Joe, ou=sales, o=acme.com	User

Information about NDS Access Control was presented in Chapter 4 and won't be repeated here.

NDS Replication

An interesting feature of NDS is the way it controls how data is replicated across the network. On each NDS server some part of the DIT is stored. NDS allows the administrator to divide the DIT up into pieces known as *partitions.* Each partition contains a subtree of the entire DIT. Each partition is stored on one or more NDS servers. The example NDS DIT from Figure 7.2 has been expanded with a few more objects below, and dotted boxes were added to show some example partitions (see Figure 7.3).

The one object in each of the three NDS partitions that is closest to the root names the partition. In this case the three partitions are

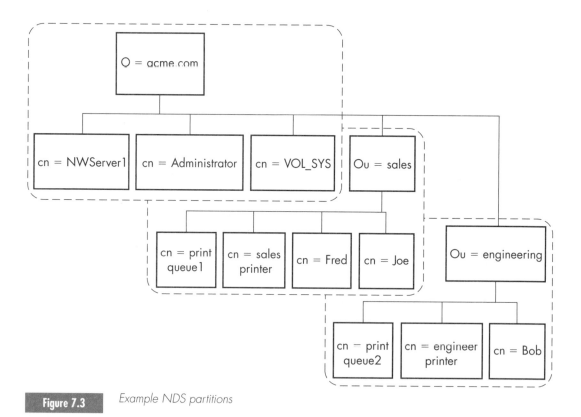

Figure 7.3   *Example NDS partitions*

- [root]
- OU=sales
- OU=engineering

A single instance of a partition is called a *replica*. Partitions can have multiple replicas. NDS servers can hold more than one replica, as long as each replica is of a different partition. One of the replicas (usually the first created) of a given partition must be designated the *master replica*. Each partition can have only one master replica; the other replicas are designated as either read-write or read-only replicas. You can use the read-only replica only to read the information in the partition. Thus, only LDAP Search operations will be directed to read-only partitions. You cannot write to a read-only partition. For example, an LDAP Modify operation cannot be implemented against a read-only replica. NDS automatically redirects the Modify operation to a writable replica. Replication adds fault tolerance to the database because the database has more than one copy of its information. Thus, even if one NDS server is down or unavailable, the NDS client can still access and possibly change data in a partition if another replica of the server's partitions is available someplace else in the network.

Synchronization is the process of ensuring that all changes to a particular partition are made to every replica of that partition. Most NDS replication is implemented using a peer-to-peer mechanism.[4] In a peer-to-peer synchronization system, updates can be made to any read-write or master replica. At a predetermined interval, all servers holding copies of the same partition communicate with each other to determine who holds the latest information for each object. The servers update their replicas with the latest information for each replica. Consider the following example. Assume that there are four NDS servers in the network, on which are stored the partitions in Table 7.2.

Notice that this layout shows two writable replicas of each partition. Each master partition is writable, just as the read-write partitions are. There are three replicas of each partition since the server NDS4 holds read-only replicas of all of the partitions. As changes are made to objects in the writable replicas, NDS synchronizes these changes to all replicas of the modified partition. NDS allows the administrator to control the interval at which information is replicated across the network. The time period between the synchronization attempts by an NDS server ranges from nearly immediately to many hours. Because the NDS must synchronize many replicas, not all replicas hold the latest changes at any given time. In other words, as soon as a change is made to NDS, all of the other replicas will hold out-of-date information until the next synchronization attempt.

---

4. Some objects in NDS are replicated using a master/slave mechanism. This replication mechanism is also used in Microsoft's ADS, where it is the primary replication mechanism.

Table 7.2	*Example of distributing partitions across NDS servers*	
NDS Server	**NDS Partition**	**Partition Type**
NDS1	[root]	Master
NDS1	OU=sales	Master
NDS1	OU=engineering	Read-write
NDS2	[root]	Read-write
NDS2	OU=sales	Read-write
NDS3	OU=engineering	Master
NDS4	[root]	Read only
NDS4	OU=sales	Read only
NDS4	OU=engineering	Read only

Assume that a change is made to the object: Cn=Joe, ou=sales, o=acme
.com on server NDS2. At the next synchronization attempt this change must be
passed on to the replicas of the OU=sales partition that is held on servers: NDS1
and NDS4. If a synchronization attempt fails because an NDS server is down or
some network connectivity failure, NDS will transmit the changes to the replicas on the affected servers, and those replicas will receive updates when the
problem is resolved. Because NDS allows changes to be made to two replicas simultaneously, NDS must resolve scenarios in which the same object is modified
on two writable replicas. If this happens, NDS will resolve the changes at the
next time that the two NDS servers attempt to synchronize.

The first thing that happens during the synchronization of two replicas is
time synchronization. Time synchronization ensures that multiple changes to
NDS are done in the order they occur and that all servers in a Directory tree report a consistent time. NDS keeps this time using Universal Time Coordinated
(UTC), which is the time at Greenwich, United Kingdom.[5] NDS needs this consistent time to establish the order of different operations done on different replicas in the Directory tree. Time synchronization may not provide the correct
time of day exactly, but it ensures that the servers in the tree remain synchronized. With time synchronization, NDS can stamp Directory events with a unique
time stamp, which identifies an event and associates it with a time. Time synchronization makes sure that all time stamps are based on the same time across
the network.

Assume that the changes are made to: Cn=Joe, ou=sales, o=acme.com.
as in Figure 7.4.

---

5. UTC is also known as Greenwich Mean Time (GMT).

- At 10:30 on NDS1 the Description attribute is deleted.
- At 10:32 on NDS2 the Description attribute is modified (using the replace suboperation) to hold the character string: "Joe sells lots of stuff."
- At 10:34 on NDS1 the Description attribute is modified (using the replace suboperation) to hold the character string: "Joe doesn't sell much stuff."
- At 10:35 on NDS2 the Description attribute is modified (using the Add suboperation) to hold the character string: "Joe is the number one salesperson."

Figure 7.4   *NDS Collision in distributed entries*

If the next synchronization attempt occurs at 10:40 between NDS1 and NDS2, the state of each partition is given in Table 7.3, assuming that previously the Description attribute held the value: "Apprentice salesperson."

Table 7.3   *Example NDS synchronization*

Time	NDS1 Description	NDS2 Description
10:30	[empty]	"Apprentice salesperson"
10:32	[empty]	"Joe sells lots of stuff."
10:34	"Joe doesn't sell much stuff."	"Joe sells lots of stuff."
10:35	"Joe doesn't sell much stuff."	"Joe sells lots of stuff."
		"Joe is the number one salesperson."
10:40	"Joe doesn't sell much stuff."	"Joe doesn't sell much stuff."
	"Joe is the number one salesperson."	"Joe is the number one salesperson."

Notice that after the first change is made to the object, each replica holds different values for the Description attribute. Also, the final result of the four changes that have been made is probably different than each administrator had expected. So, even though NDS has applied all of the changes in the exact order in which they were entered, the end result is that the Description attribute holds information that looks unusual to humans but absolutely correct to NDS. Thus even though NDS has sophisticated Time synchronization and data synchronization mechanisms, external administrative controls must be in place when a complex distributed NDS infrastructure is deployed. In the example above, the NDS1 and NDS2 administrators must contact each other and resolve the value of Joe's Description attribute manually and then modify the attribute value again as appropriate.

PART THREE

Building LDAP Programs Using Java

CHAPTER OBJECTIVES

Language bindings are available for LDAP APIs in a wide variety of programming languages. However, Java is of significant interest because of the wide variety of environments in which it can be used. There are three main classes of programs that can be built using Java. Java Applications are standard types of programs and run on any operating system to which the Java Virtual Machine has been ported, such as Windows, UNIX, and numerous wireless devices, such as those that support the Palm OS. Java Applets are programs that run within the environment created by a Web Browser, such as Netscape Navigator or Microsoft's Internet Explorer. Java places special restrictions on the types of functions that can be implemented in an Applet. Java Servlets are programs that run on a Java Application Server. The start of a Servlet is initiated by the action of a Web Browser, but unlike an Applet, a Servlet runs on the machine from which the Web page was downloaded. Because Servlets run in the environment of the Web server, they provide a mechanism for extending the functionality of a Web server. They do this by allowing the Web pages to hold dynamic content that can change each time the Web page is viewed.

Java is not the only programming language that allows the developer to write programs that can be deployed in these three environments:

- Operating System Desktop
- Web Browser
- Web Server

For each of the above environments, there are successful, competing technologies to Java. For example, Active Server Page (ASP) technology presents a viable alternative to Java Servlets. It is straightforward to integrate LDAP into ASP technology. Java is used here because it provides a more cohesive way of addressing the different environments with a single solution, not because it provides a substantially superior solution to any one of the three environments above. This chapter assumes that the reader has a working knowledge of Java and LDAP.

LDAP APIs for Java

There are two APIs that are available for writing LDAP programs in Java. Javasoft provides that Java Naming and Directory Interface (JNDI) as part of its standard distribution of Java in the Java 2 Enterprise Edition (J2EE) version of Java.[1] A competing interface that originated from the Netscape LDAP Software Development Kit (SDK) for Java is also available.[2] This API is in the process of being standardized by the IETF and should be available as an RFC by the time this book is published. This SDK is now made available as part of the Mozilla open source project at *www.mozilla.org*. There are slight differences between the original Netscape API, the current Mozilla API, and the API to be approved by the IETF. However, the core of the API used in this book is the same. This API could easily be referred to as the Netscape API, the Mozilla API, or even the IETF API. For the purposes of this book, it will be referred to as simply the Netscape API, since that identifies its origins. While there are slight differences between these three versions, the core of the specifications are identical, and there are no differences in the portions of the APIs used here.

Both of these APIs work equally well with NDS and Active Directory. The Netscape API is a purely LDAP API that works as an LDAP client. On the other hand, JNDI is a "pluggable" API that works as an LDAP client as well as having the ability to act as a client to other kinds of Directory services (e.g., DNS), such as the Domain Name Service. JNDI is called pluggable, since different "service providers" can be plugged into its framework. In addition to the LDAP and DNS service providers, there are also other third-party service providers that work

---

1. An excellent reference for JNDI is *The JNDI Tutorial and Reference* by Rosanna Lee and Scott Seligman (Boston: Addison-Wesley, 2000).
2. An excellent reference for the Netscape LDAP API for Java is *LDAP Programming with Java* by Rob Weltman and Tony Dahbura (Boston: Addison-Wesley, 2000).

with JNDI. For example, Novell has created a JNDI service provider for NDS that exposes some NDS specific features that are not available in other LDAP servers such as Active Directory.

While both APIs provide similar features for writing LDAP client applications, I believe that the Netscape API provides a more straightforward implementation for LDAP developers. Its connection model compares favorably to the JNDI context model. The discussion of this chapter will focus on the use of the Netscape API, and the examples in the following chapter will make use of this API. However, it is straightforward to implement the examples in the following chapter in JNDI, and programmers with experience with JNDI should have no problem doing so. As a reference, the Javadoc specification of the Netscape API may be found at *www.mozilla.com*.

The Netscape LDAP API for Java

There are several packages that make up the API. The two that are of primary interest are

- netscape.ldap. The main package, which includes methods for executing all of the LDAP operations, for example, Bind, Search, and so forth
- netscape.ldap.util. An auxiliary pack that includes various useful utility classes, such as manipulating DNs

In the standard distribution, most classes are built into the ldapjdk.jar Java archive. In most situations, this is the only jar file that needs to be distributed with your LDAP program. When using the Netscape API, the programmer needs to map the LDAP operations that are being used into the methods that are available in the API. This section introduces the essentials of the API and provides enough of a foundation to implement the example applications in the following chapter. It definitely does not provide a detailed explanation of all of the methods and fields that are available in each class that is part of the API.

Connecting to the LDAP Server

The first step in any LDAP program is the creation of a logical connection to the LDAP server. While LDAPv3 does not specifically require a Bind operation to be the first operation submitted over the connection, it is good practice to do so. Even when your program will be using an anonymous authentication, it is important to create a valid connection and to initiate a Bind. This is because many administrators configure their LDAP servers to refuse to handle operations that are submitted over unauthenticated connections. The Netscape API has a class called *LDAPConnection* that must be instantiated in order to create this connection. The most common constructor that is used for objects of this class is the default constructor that takes no parameters. The LDAPConnection object

```
{
  String hostname = "ldap.dtasi.com";
  String myDN = "uid=admin, o=dtasi.com";
  String myPassword = "xyzzy";

  LDAPConnection myConnection = new LDAPConnection();
  try {
    myConnection.connect(hostname, 389);
    myConnection.authenticate( myDN, myPassword );
    ...
  } catch (LDAPException e) {
    System.out.println("Bind failed, error is "
    + e.toString());
  }
  ...
}
```

Figure 8.1	*Simple Bind to an LDAP server over a TCP connection*

represents a valid socket connection to an LDAP server. The socket can be either a TCP socket (the default socket) or an SSL socket. In order to connect the socket to an LDAP server, the *connect* method is used. Normally, the connect method takes the hostname and port number as arguments.

Once the connection is created, it can then be used to issue any LDAP operations. The Bind, the first operation that is used, is initiated by invoking the *authenticate* method of the LDAPConnection class. So, typical code for creating the connection to the server and issuing a Bind operation is as in Figure 8.1.

This code creates a TCP connection to the LDAP server named "ldap.dtasi .com" and then issues a Bind operation using the DN "uid=admin, o=dtasi.com" and the password "xyzzy." Version 4.1 of the Netscape SDK includes the capability to use an alternate constructor for the LDAPConnection class. This alternate constructor, which accepts a single parameter that specifies a "socket factory," is Netscape's mechanism for including support for SSL connections. A socket factory is any class that implements the *LDAPSocketFactory* interface. The standard class that is provided that implements this interface is the *SSLSocketFactory* class. SSLSocketFactory is part of the Java Secure Socket Extension (JSSE) API from Javasoft. JSSE is a set of Java packages that enable secure Internet communications. It implements a Java version of SSL and includes features for data encryption, message digests, and digital signatures. Using JSSE, developers can provide for the secure passage of data between a client and a server running any application protocol, including LDAP. JSSE will be provided as a standard feature of the Java 2 SDK version 1.4 and is part of the javax.net.ssl package. It is very easy to get an SSLSocketFactory by calling the static *getDefault* method of SSLSocketFactory. So, in order to create an SSL socket for the connection to the LDAP server, the code in Figure 8.1 can be modified as in Figure 8.2.

In connecting to either NDS or Active Directory, there must be a matching set of encryption algorithms configured for both the client side and the

```
{
  String hostname = "ldap.dtasi.com";
  String myDN = "uid=admin, o=dtasi.com";
  String myPassword = "xyzzy";

  SocketFactory myFactory =
    SSLSocketFactory.getDefault();
  LDAPConnection myConnection = new
    LDAPConnection(myFactory);
  try {
    myConnection.connect(hostname, 663);
    myConnection.authenticate( myDN, myPassword );
    ...
  } catch (LDAPException e) {
    int errCode = e.getLDAPResultCode();
    System.out.println("Bind failed, error is "
      + errCode + ": " + e.toString());
  }
  ...
}
```

| Figure 8.2 | *Simple Bind to an LDAP server over an SSL connection* |

server side. Much configuration and trial and error will be in order for each new installation.

Searching the Directory

Once the connection to the Directory has been established, Search and other operations can be performed. The standard *search* method of the LDAP-Connection class is used, and the normal format takes the same parameters as the LDAP Search operation. These parameters are

- base. DN of the starting point in the DIT for the search
- scope. Either subtree, object only or container only
- filter. The specification of the search criteria
- attrs. The list of attributes to be returned (null returns all attributes)
- attrsOnly. Boolean indication of whether values should be returned (this is normally false so that values are returned; otherwise, only attribute names are returned)

The *LDAPv2* interface of the API provides the constants that can be used for the scope field. Note that the use of the LDAPv2 Java interface does not imply that we are using an "LDAP version 2" connect. The LDAPv2 interface is just where the needed constants are defined. The version of LDAP being used can be set in the authenticate method and defaults to 3. They are

- LDAPv2.SCOPE_SUB
- LDAPv2.SCOPE_BASE
- LDAPv2.SCOPE_ONE

```
String mySearchbase = "o=dtasi.com";
String myFilter="(objectclass=person)";
LDAPSearchResults myResults = null;
try {
  myResults = myConnection.search( mySearchbase,
    LDAPv2.SCOPE_SUB, myFilter, null, false );
} catch ( LDAPException e ) {
    int errCode = e.getLDAPResultCode();
    System.out.println("Bind failed, error is "
      + errCode + ": " + e.toString());
}
```

Figure 8.3   *Subtree search*

The LDAPv2 interface is used just to access these constants, which does not imply that version 2 of LDAP is being used. Thus, in order to perform a subtree search from "o=dtasi.com" for entries with the object class of person, the call in Figure 8.3 would be made.

Notice in the search filter that there are no spaces. In theory, spaces are allowed in the search filter for readability. However, it is better to remove them, since LDAP servers may have difficulty parsing the search filter with spaces present. Once the Search operation has been submitted, the next step is to collect the results. The results are returned in the LDAPSearchResults structure. An LDAPSearchResults structure is really just a collection of LDAPEntry objects. An LDAPEntry object is in turn really just a collection of LDAPAttribute objects. The retrieval of information from the LDAPSearchResults structure is shown in Figure 8.4.

Calling the search method and retrieving the results using other scopes is similar. The only change that needs to be made is in the case when the scope field is set to LDAPv2.SCOPE_ONE. In this scenario, only one LDAPEntry object in the LDAPSearchResults object is created as a result of the call to the search method. So, there is no need to have the outer while loop as seen in Figure 8.4. Other than that one change, the code is always the same for the retrieval of search results. The LDAPAttributeSet class does have a method *getAttribute* that takes a string so that specific attributes can be retrieved by name. This allows the developer to short-circuit the while loop. Except in situations where only one or two attributes are needed from the entry, it is best to leave the attrs parameter to the search method as null. Even though this may generate excess network traffic for some additional data transfer, the code is much simpler and is less likely to generate an error on the server. The errors may occur if the entry in question does not have a requested attribute or the authenticated user does not have appropriate access to retrieve the requested attribute.

Adding Entries

Adding entries to the Directory is basically the opposite of searching the Directory. Instead of retrieving LDAPEntry objects from the Directory and pulling the

```
while ( myResults.hasMoreElements() ) {
  LDAPEntry myEntry = myResults.next();
  String nextDN = myEntry.getDN();
  System.out.println( nextDN );
  LDAPAttributeSet entryAttrs =
    myEntry.getAttributeSet();
  Enumeration attrs = entryAttrs.getAttributes();
  while ( attrs.hasMoreElements() ) {
    LDAPAttribute attr = (LDAPAttribute)
      attrs.nextElement();
    String attrName = attr.getName();
    System.out.println( "\t" + attrName + ":" );
    Enumeration vals = attr.getStringValues();
    while ( vals.hasMoreElements() ) {
      String nextValue = (String) vals.nextElement();
      System.out.println( "\t\t" + nextValue );
    }
  }
}
```

Figure 8.4   *Retrieval of search results*

attributes out, LDAPEntry objects are created from scratch and then pushed into the Directory. In order to add an entry to the Directory, the *add* method of the LDAPConnection class is used. The code to add an organizational unit entry underneath the "o=dtasi.com" entry is shown in Figure 8.5.

Notice that the same LDAPConnection object is being used as before. Attributes are added one at a time to the LDAPAttributeSet object. Some attributes, such as the objectClass attribute, have multiple values that are held in the LDAPAttribute object. Once all of the attributes have been added to the LDAPAttributeSet, the LDAPEntry object is created using the LDAPAttributeSet object and a DN. This entry is passed as the only parameter to the add method. Notice that the LDAPException object has defined constants for the various result codes that may be returned from the LDAP operations. In this case, a special consideration is made for the situation in which an entry already exists in the Directory with the DN of "ou=sales, o=dtasi.com." In normal coding situations, you may want to catch a wide variety of exceptions in this manner.

Modifying Entries

Modifying entries is very similar to adding entries. In this case, instead of creating an LDAPEntry object, an LDAPModificationSet object is created. This object lists the changes that are to be made to an existing entry in the Directory. In order to modify an entry in the Directory, the *modify* method of the LDAPConnection class is used. Consider the situation in Figure 8.6, in which we want to change the description attribute of the "ou=sales" entry that was just created above.

Notice that a different constructor is used for the LDAPAttribute class in creating the attrDescription object. This constructor specifies the attribute type

```
String parentOrg = "o=dtasi.com"
String ouName = "sales";
String ouDescription = "the sales organization";
String dn;
dn = "ou=" + ouName + ", " + parentOrg;
// Specify the attributes of the entry
String objectclass_values[] = { "top",
  "organizationalUnit" };
LDAPAttributeSet attrs = new LDAPAttributeSet();
LDAPAttribute attr = new LDAPAttribute( "objectclass" );
for( int i = 0; i < objectclass_values.length; i++ ) {
  if (objectclass_values[i].length() > 0)
    attr.addValue( objectclass_values[i] );
}
attrs.add( attr );
attr = new LDAPAttribute( "description" );
attr.addValue( ouDescription );
attrs.add( attr );

// Create an entry with this DN and these attributes
LDAPEntry myEntry = new LDAPEntry( dn, attrs );
try {
  // Now add the entry to the directory
  myConnection.add( myEntry );
}
catch( LDAPException e ) {
  if ( e.getLDAPResultCode() ==
    LDAPException.ENTRY_ALREADY_EXISTS )
    System.out.println("Error: Entry already present\n"
      );
  else
    System.out.println( "Error: " + e.toString()
      + "\n");
}
```

Figure 8.5 *Code to add an entry to the Directory*

as "description" and the value of the attribute. Notice that the modify operation that is used in this scenario is the REPLACE operation. The LDAPModification class has constants defined for ADD and DELETE as well. If other changes to the entry were desired, then they would be added to the LDAPModificationSet object as well. In this case, only one change needs to be made. Once all changes have been collected in the LDAPModificationSet object, it is passed as a parameter to the modify method along with the DN of the entry to be changed.

Deleting Entries

Deleting an entry from the Directory is easy. All that you need to do is to call the *delete* method of the LDAPConnection class. Pass is the only parameter in the DN of the entry to be deleted (see Figure 8.7).

```
LDAPModificationSet mods = new LDAPModificationSet();
LDAPAttribute attrDescription =
  new LDAPAttribute( "description",
    "the sales organization of dtasi.com" );
mods.add( LDAPModification.REPLACE, attrDescription);
String entryToChange  "ou=sales,o=dtasi.com";
try {
  myConnection.modify(entryToChange, mods );
}
catch( LDAPException e ) {
  System.out.println( "Error: " e.toString()
    + "\n" );
}
```

Figure 8.6   *Code to modify an entry in the Directory*

```
String entryToDelete  "ou=sales,o=dtasi.com";
try {
  myConnection.delete(entryToDelete );
}
catch( LDAPException e ) {
  if ( e.getLDAPResultCode() ==
    LDAPException.NOT_ALLOWED_ON_NONLEAF)
    System.out.println("Error: OU isn't empty!\n");
  else
    System.out.println( "Error: " e.toString()
      + "\n" );
}
```

Figure 8.7   *Code to delete an entry in the Directory*

If somehow the "ou=sales" container isn't empty, then the delete operation will fail, and an exception will be thrown. This particular error is caught using the NOT_ALLOWED_ON_NONLEAF constant defined in the LDAPException class.

Using Compare

While the LDAP compare is not used as often as other operations, it does have useful functions, especially to check for group membership and to see whether a supplied password is accurate. Checking the password may not be possible in many installations as access controls may be in place to disallow this function. Checking group membership is always a possibility. The compare operation is implemented using the *compare* method of the LDAPConnection class. Note that JNDI does not specifically support the compare operation. Instead, programmers are advised to use an equivalent search method. In the example in Figure 8.8, a group "cn=field sales, ou=sales, o=dtasi.com" is checked to see if the user "uid=bgreenblatt, o=dtasi.com" is a member.

```
String myDN = "cn=field sales, ou=sales, o=dtasi.com";
String attrName = "member";
DN userDN = new DN("uid=bgreenblatt,o=dtasi.com");
String attrVal = userDN.toRFCString();
LDAPAttribute compareAttr = new
  LDAPAttribute(attrName, attrVal);
try {
  boolean groupMember =
    myConnection.compare(myDN, compareAttr);
  if (groupMember) {
    System.out.println(
      "bgreenblatt is a member of the group." );
  } else {
    System.out.println(
      "bgreenblatt is not a member of the group." );
  }
} catch ( LDAPException e ) {
  if ( e.getLDAPResultCode() ==
    System.out.println( "Error: " e.toString()
      + "\n" );
}
```

| Figure 8.8 | *Code to use the compare method to check group membership* |

Notice that the DN class is used in this code segment to check for values. The DN class is found in the *netscape.ldap.util* package. It is always good practice to use this class to specify strings that are DN values that are to be stored in the Directory. The *toRFCString* method of the DN class insures that the string is formatted correctly according to RFC 2253. The DN class includes many useful methods for manipulating DNs, including *getParent* and *explodeDN*. The get-Parent method returns another DN object, which is logically one step up in the DIT. For example, using the value assigned to the *myDN* variable in the above code segment, getParent(myDN) would return the DN with the string representation of "ou=sales, o=dtasi.com." The explodeDN method returns an array of strings that represent each RDN in the DN. For example, again using the value assigned to the *myDN* variable in the above code segment, explodeDN(myDN) would return an array with the three values ["cn=field sales," "ou=sales," "o=dtasi.com"].

This package also includes an RDN class with useful methods for dealing with DN components. The most useful methods in the RDN class are *toString* and *isRDN*. The toString method returns the string representation of the RDN. The isRDN method is a static method of the class that returns a Boolean indication of whether a specified string is a valid RDN.

Renaming Entries

In LDAP Directory entries can be renamed by using the rename method of the LDAPConnection class. The rename method corresponds to the LDAP modify-

```
DN oldSalesEntryDN = new DN("ou=sales, o=dtasi.com");
RDN newSalesEntryRDN = new RDN("ou=dtasi sales ");
try {
  myConnection.rename(oldSalesEntryDN.toRFCString(),
    newSalesEntryRDN.toString(), true );
} catch ( LDAPException e ) {
  if ( e.getLDAPResultCode() ==
    System.out.println( "Error: " e.toString()
      + "\n" );
}
```

Figure 8.9   *Code to rename the "ou=sales" entry*

RDN operation. The code segment in Figure 8.9 renames the "ou=sales" entry to "ou=dtasi sales."

In the code, the third parameter is deleteOldRDN and represents the Boolean instruction of whether to keep the old RDN (in this case, "ou=sales") as an attribute value of the new entry. In this case, it is set to true so that the new entry will not have a multivalued ou attribute.

Using Asynchronous Commands

Most operations in the Netscape SDK are accomplished using synchronous calls. What this means is that the SDK will not return a result to the calling application until the LDAP server has returned results to the client. Thus, the application will wait, and there is no possibility of abandoning an outstanding operation. The Netscape SDK also has facilities for operating in asynchronous mode. In this case, the calls return immediately without waiting for the server to return the actual results of the operation. Coding using asynchronous calls is substantially more complex than the synchronous calls used in all of the previous examples.

Asynchronous calls differ from their corresponding synchronous versions by the addition of a listener parameter in each method. In the case of search operations, the listener class is *LDAPSearchListener.* The LDAPSearchListener objects help to manage the search results, referrals, and exceptions that come back to the client as a result of search operations that have been submitted to the server. The responses that have been returned can be retrieved at the clients' convenience by calling the *getResponse* method, which returns an LDAPMessage object. The LDAPMessage object corresponds to the LDAPMessage ASN.1 structure that is defined in the LDAP protocol specification. In the case of a search result, a subclass of LDAPMessage called LDAPSearchResult is used. This class adds the method *getEntry,* which returns the LDAPEntry associated with that search result. Remember that each entry in the results of a search is returned in a separate search result message. Once the LDAPEntry object is retrieved from the listener, it can be manipulated in the same way as in the synchronous example.

```
try {
  LDAPConnection[] ld = new LDAPConnection[3];
  String[] hosts = { "foo1", "foo2", "foo3" };
  int[] ports = { 389, 389, 2018 }
  String[] bases = { "o=Airius.com", "o=Acme.com",
    "dc=Acme,dc=com" };
  // search for all entries with surname of Jensen
  String MY_FILTER = "sn=Jensen";

  for( int i = 0; i < ld.length; i++ ) {
    ld[i] = new LDAPConnection();
    ld[i].connect( hosts[i], ports[i] );
  }
  // Get a response listener for one search
  // notice that passing null indicates that we need a
  // new listener

  LDAPSearchListener l =
    ld[0].search( bases[0], ld.SCOPE_SUB,
      MY_FILTER, null, false,
      (LDAPSearchListener) null );

  // Share the listener with the other connections
    for( i = 1; i < ld.length; i++ ) {
      ld[i].search( bases[i], ld[i].SCOPE_SUB,
        MY_FILTER, null, false, l );
    }

  LDAPMessage msg;
  while( (msg = l.getResponse()) != null ) {
    if ( msg instanceof LDAPSearchResultReference ) {
        String[] urls =
          ((LDAPSearchResultReference)msg).getUrls();
          // Do something with the referrals...
    } else if ( msg instanceof LDAPSearchResult ) {
        LDAPEntry entry =
          ((LDAPSearchResult) msg).getEntry();
      // The rest of the processing is the same as for
      // a synchronous search
        System.out.println( entry.getDN() );
    } else {
      // A search response
        LDAPResponse res = (LDAPResponse)msg;
        int status = res.getResultCode();
        if ( status == LDAPException.SUCCESS ) {
      // Nothing to do
          } else {
            String err =
```

Figure 8.10 *Using asynchronous calls*

```
                LDAPException.errorCodeToString(status);
             throw new LDAPException( err, status,
                res.getErrorMessage(),
                res.getMatchedDN() );
          }
        }
      }
   } catch ( LDAPException e ) {
      System.err.println( e.toString() );
   }
```

Figure 8.10   *Using asynchronous calls (continued)*

Asynchronous calls are especially useful in multithreaded applications. In these types of applications, multiple threads can issue LDAP requests, and any thread in the application can retrieve the results. Asynchronous calls are also useful when searches must be sent to multiple servers, and the results combined to form the information to be displayed to the user. The example in Figure 8.10, which is slightly modified from one in the *Netscape Directory SDK Programmer's Guide,*[3] shows how to perform a search on more than one server using the Asynchronous interface.

The getResponse call in the code above returns null only when all operations that are associated with the listener object have been completed or abandoned. If no results are available yet, the call blocks until some results have been returned from the server. In code that is multithreaded, it may be desirable to abandon outstanding searches. This is done using the *abandon* method of the LDAPConnection object. In its simplest form, the abandon method takes a single parameter that is an LDAPSearchListener object. This version abandons all outstanding searches that are being managed by that listener.

Ending the Connection

Once all work is completed with the LDAP server, the LDAPConnection object should be disconnected. Note that the creation of an LDAPConnection object is relatively expensive, and it should be reused if possible. Unfortunately, there is no specific method to "unbind" from the server. An unbind request can be sent to the server using the LDAPConnection's *disconnect* method, which takes no parameter. However, if a new bind method is issued on an existing authenticated LDAPConnection object, this will have the same effect as an unbind. So, if you want to save a connection for later use and don't want to leave an authenticated connection laying around, an anonymous bind can be issued, which

---

3. *Netscape Directory SDK 4.0 for Java Programmer's Guide,* © 1999 by Netscape Communications Corp.

will discard the current authentication information but will leave open the connection to the server.

Using LDAP in Java Applets

Java Applets operate with special security restrictions that impact the ability to use LDAP within the browser context. The meaningful restriction for LDAP programmers is that Applets can open socket connections only to the same host and port from which the Applet was downloaded. This means that, unless the Web server also understands LDAP requests, Java Applets are restricted from issuing LDAP requests. Since no Web server also understands LDAP, this is a serious problem. Fortunately, there are ways around this restriction. Each Web Browser implements a security model in which an Applet can ask permission to breach one of the security restrictions. Netscape defined extensions to version 1.1 of the JDK that allow the Applet to request these same capabilities. These extensions are contained in the *Netscape Capabilities* classes. One such capability that can be requested is the *UniversalConnect* privilege that allows the Applet to connect to any other network server, instead of just the server from which the Applet was loaded. The line of code shown in Figure 8.11 implements this call.

When the Web Browser executes this line of code, it causes a dialog box to be displayed to allow the user to grant or deny this request. Figure 8.12 shows this dialog.

If the user presses the *Grant* button then the program can continue execution. If the user presses the *Deny* button then the Applet is not allowed to connect, and a Java runtime exception is raised. Notice that this panel has a button with the title *Certificate*. This button is present because the compiled Java code is stored on the Web server in the form of a digitally signed Java archive (JAR) file. Pressing the *Certificate* button will display certain information from the Certificate of the signer of the JAR file, such as the name of the signer, the issuing authority for the certificate, and an email address.

Microsoft has defined a virtually identical mechanism for use in the Internet Explorer (IE) Browser. These calls are from the Microsoft Security API. Microsoft does not use JAR files for IE. Instead cabinet files are used, which must also be digitally signed for use with the security API. A simple class that encapsulates this API is shown in Figure 8.13.

New to Java 2 is yet another security model that allows for a similar but

```
netscape.security.PrivilegeManager.enablePrivilege
    ("UniversalConnect");
```

Figure 8.11   *Request for the Applet to connect to an Internet site other than the one from which the Applet was loaded*

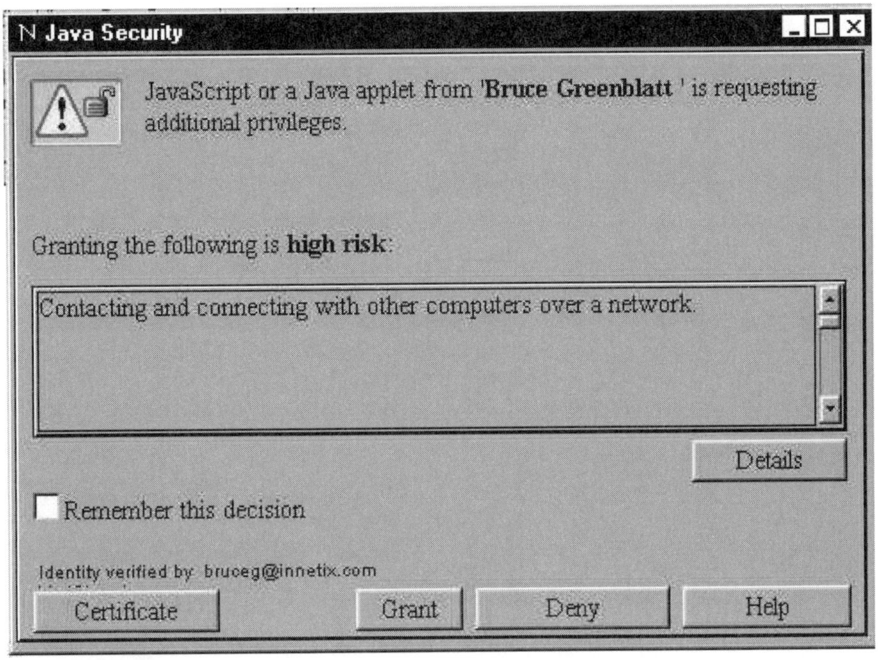

Figure 8.12 *Dialog to allow the user to grant or deny UniversalConnect privilege*

more complex method of requesting permission to access the network. The new permission request mechanism could also be encapsulated using the above classes, but those new mechanisms won't be discussed in this text.[4] Consider the code in Figure 8.14, which implements an Applet using the above class.

This Applet is very simple. It has three text fields that allow a user to enter a server name, a user ID, and a password. The Applet collects this information and uses it to attempt to bind to a server. Notice that prior to connecting to the LDAP server, the Applet first asks permission by calling the setNetworkPermission method in the permission class that we defined above.

Using LDAP in Servlets

Using LDAP in Servlets is very simple and has no restrictions. Since the code in a Servlet is running on the machine from which the Web page was downloaded,

---

4. For more information about the Java 2 security model, an excellent reference is *Securing Java* by Gary McGraw and Edward Felten (New York: John Wiley & Sons, 1999).

```
import com.ms.security.*;

/* The setPermissions class is used to encapsulate the
   Applet security mechanism for Internet Explorer.
      In order to access the network from inside an Applet
      these methods can be called. It also allows for easy
      modification to allow use from the Netscape browser.
      Only the code in this file needs to be changed when
      the Applet security model is changed.
*/

public class setPermissions {

  /* The setNetworkPermission method asks for
     permission to access an arbitrary network host.
   */

  public void setNetworkPermission () {
    PolicyEngine.assertPermission(PermissionID.NETIO);
  }

  /* The setSystemPermission method asks for permission
     to access any system resource, not just the
     network.
   */

  public void setSystemPermission () {
    PolicyEngine.assertPermission(PermissionID.SYSTEM);
  }
}
```

Figure 8.13   *Microsoft Security API for requesting permission to make LDAP connections*

```
public class LDAPApplet extends Applet
{
  java.awt.TextField LDAPServerTextField;
  java.awt.Label LDAPServerLabel;
  java.awt.TextField nameTextField;
  java.awt.Label nameLabel;
  java.awt.TextField passwordTextField;
  java.awt.Label passwordLabel;
  java.awt.Button okButton;
  setPermissions myPermissions;
  LDAPConnection myConnection;

  public LDAPApplet ()
  {
```

Figure 8.14   *Simple Applet containing LDAP code to connect to a server*

```
setLayout(new GridLayout(4,2,5,5));
// 4 rows 2 columns
setSize(430,430);
LDAPServerTextField = new java.awt.TextField();
LDAPServerTextField.setSize(156,24);
add(LDAPServerTextField);
LDAPServerLabel = new java.awt.Label("LDAP Server");
LDAPServerLabel.setSize(100,24);
add(LDAPServerLabel);
nameTextField = new java.awt.TextField();
nameTextField.setSize(156,24);
add(nameTextField);
nameLabel = new java.awt.Label("Name");
nameLabel.setSize(100,24);
add(nameLabel);
passwordTextField = new java.awt.TextField();
passwordTextField.setSize(156,24);
add(passwordTextField);
passwordLabel = new java.awt.Label("Password");
passwordLabel.setSize(100,24);
add(passwordLabel);
okButton = new java.awt.Button();
okButton.setLabel("OK");
okButton.setSize(60,40);
okButton.addActionListener(new okButtonListener());
add(okButton);
passwordTextField.setEchoChar('*');
myPermissions = new setPermissions();
}

class okButtonListener implements ActionListener {

  public void actionPerformed(ActionEvent event) {
      LDAPApplet myParent = (LDAPApplet) getParent();
      String password = passwordTextField.getText();

      String name = nameTextField.getText();
      String serverName =
        LDAPServerTextField.getText();
      try {
        myPermissions.setNetworkPermission();
        myConnection = new LDAPConnection();
        myPermissions.setNetworkPermission();
        myConnection.connect( serverName, 389 );
        myConnection.authenticate( name, password );
      } catch ( LDAPException e) {
        myParent.showStatus
        ("Unable to connect to the LDAP Server.\n"
         + "Please try again\n");
```

Figure 8.14   *Simple Applet containing LDAP code to connect to a server (continued)*

```
            myParent.showStatus ("Exception is " +
             e.toString() +"\n");
            return;
        } catch ( Exception e) {
        myParent.showStatus
            ("Unable to connect to the LDAP Server.\n"
             + "Non LDAP error. Please try again\n");
        myParent.showStatus ("Exception is " +
            e.toString() +"\n");
        return;
        }
      }
    }
  }
```

Figure 8.14   *Simple Applet containing LDAP code to connect to a server (continued)*

```html
<html>
<head>
<title>JWare Login Screen</title>
<meta http-equiv="Content-Type" content="text/html;
charset=iso-8859-1">
</head>

<body bgcolor="#FFFFFF" >
<form name="form1" method="post" action="login_Servlet">
  <p>Server
    <input id="serverField" type="text" name="Server">
  </p>
  <p>User ID
    <input id="useridField" type="text" name="UserID">
  </p>
  <p>Password
    <input id="password" type="password"
     name="Password">
  </p>
  <p>
    <input id="loginButton" type="submit" name="Login"
     value="Login">
  </p>
</form>
</body>
</html>
```

Figure 8.15   *HTML form for collecting LDAP Bind information*

not inside the Web Browser, there are no security restrictions. Thus, a Servlet that makes use of LDAP is free to open a connection to any server on the Internet. Consider the Hypertext Markup Language (HTML) form in Figure 8.15 that can be used to input the necessary login data.

The action field of the form tag mentions the name of the Servlet that will be used to process the form. Application servers such as Tomcat will automatically process the form using the appropriate Servlet. The code to process the form is pretty straightforward (see Figure 8.16).

```
public class login_Servlet extends HttpServlet {

  public login_1Servlet() {
  }

  public void doPost(HttpServletRequest request,
   HttpServletResponse response)
   throws IOException, ServletException
  {
    String myServer = request.getParameter("Server");
    String myUserid = request.getParameter("UserID");
    String myPassword =
      request.getParameter("Password");
    LDAPConnection myConnection = new LDAPConnection();
    try {
      myConnection.connect( ldapHostName, 389 );
      myConnection.authenticate( myUserid, myPassword );
      status = new String("Login Successful");
    } catch (LDAPException e) {
      status = e.toString();
    }

    response.setContentType("text/html");
    PrintWriter out = response.getWriter();
    out.println("<html>");
    out.println("<body>");
    out.println("<head>");
    out.println("<title>Hello LDAP!</title>");
    out.println("</head>");
    out.println("<body>");
    out.println("<h1>" + status + "</h1>");
    out.println("</body>");
    out.println("</html>");
  }
}
```

Figure 8.16   *Servlet using LDAP to authenticate*

Since the form tag mentioned that the method to process the form is a post, then the application server will call the servlet's doPost method. This method simply collects the appropriate data as parameters in the HTTP request information. This information is then used to attempt to bind to the specified LDAP server. The result of the attempt is then printed out on the Browser.

Example LDAP Applications

CHAPTER OBJECTIVES

The previous chapters laid the foundation for building applications that make significant use of LDAP. This chapter follows through on that foundation and provides several in-depth examples of these types of applications taken from the real work of LDAP application developers. The first example application shows how LDAP can be used to store user and application configuration information. The second example shows how LDAP can be used for storing application-defined access control information. The third example shows how to create an LDAP-enabled mailing list administration program. Finally, we show what tasks need to be performed in order to install an LDAP-enabled application program.

All of these example applications will work with both Active Directory and NDS. Any special considerations that must be taken into account for these installations will be noted. Most of these applications will be shown using the Java LDAP API being developed as an RFC that was described in Chapter 8. It is important to note that it is possible to write LDAP applications in a wide variety of programming languages. For example, there are language bindings in C, C++, and Visual Basic. Microsoft's Active Directory Services Interface (ADSI) is an API that can be used with both NDS and Active Directory. Netscape has produced a language binding for Perl using its PerlLDAP module. This interface is becoming widely used in many scripting environments. It is even possible to use Cobol to access LDAP information in IBM's mainframe environment.

Using LDAP to Store User Configuration Information

Most applications need to keep track of some information on a user-by-user basis. Often, this information is related to user preferences for the application. Other information is personal information about the user, such as email address, postal address, and so forth. Thus, some of the personal information may already be captured in the user's LDAP entry, and the application configuration information needs only to augment the user's information that is already kept in the Directory. Additionally, LDAP can be used to store configuration information that is common to an entire organization or subtree. One solution to this problem is to define an auxiliary object class that can be used to augment users, organizational units, or organizations. The definition of this auxiliary object class will depend upon the particular application that is storing this information.

Consider an application that allows employees to order corporate clothing. For each employee, the application needs to know various sizes and colors of the clothing. For each organizational unit, the application needs to know what (if any) special clothing types are available. For the entire organization, the application needs to know the location of the logo files for use in creating the specially designed clothing. These configuration parameters can be represented using the following LDAP object class definitions. In defining these object classes, we will first assign OIDs. The OID 1.3.6.1.4.1 has been assigned as IANA-registered Private Enterprises, and IANA has assigned 5515 to Directory Tools and Application Services, Inc. (DTASI). Thus, the OID 1.3.6.1.4.1.5515 is the root OID for all DTASI-assigned OIDs. For the examples in this book, we will use the OID 1.3.6.1.4.1.5515.6 as the root OID. The object class used to hold the user configuration information can be defined as

```
( 1.3.6.1.4.1.5515.6.1.1 NAME 'exampleUserConfiguration'
SUP top
AUXILIARY MUST (shirtSize $ shirtGender $ jacketSize $
jacketGender))
```

Similarly, the object class that is used to hold the organizational configuration information can be defined as

```
( 1.3.6.1.4.1.5515.6.1.2 NAME 'exampleOrganization-
Configuration' SUP top
AUXILIARY MUST logoFileLocation)
```

We will define all of the attributes in these object classes as single valued and type *caseIgnore strings*. A sample definition is

```
(1.3.6.1.4.1.5515.6.2.1 NAME 'shirtSize' EQUALITY case-
IgnoreMatch
SYNTAX 1.3.6.1.4.1.1466.115.121.1.15 )
```

All of the other attribute types will have identical definitions, except that they will be assigned different OIDs. Representing this information as a Java class is straightforward. For each attribute type defined in the user configuration, there is a field defined in the class. For each field in the class, the standard accessor and mutator methods are defined. In Java, accessor methods are used to obtain information about an object. In the *CorporateClothing* class that is defined below, the accessor methods are

- getShirtSize(). Line 160
- getShirtGender. Line 156
- getJacketSize. Line 144
- getJacketGender. Line 140
- getLd. Line 148
- getLogoFileLocation. Line 152

Similarly, Java uses mutator methods to change information about an object. In this class, six mutator methods correspond to the same six fields to which the accessor methods correspond:

- setShirtSize(). Line 185
- setShirtGender. Line 181
- setJacketSize. Line 168
- setJacketGender. Line 164
- setLd. Line 171
- setLogoFileLocation. Line 176

Notice that these mutators do not actually change the configuration that is stored in the Directory. No changes are made via LDAP until the *storeConfig-InLDAP* method is called. A constructor is defined that takes the DN of the user that holds for which configuration information is desired. The constructor fetches the configuration information via LDAP and stores it in the fields. Notice that the constructor fetches the user configuration fields from the object named in the userNameDN parameter. However, the organizational configuration information is read from the named object's parent entry. For this example, we inspect only the parent object for the logoFileLocation attribute. In a real implementation, it may be desirable to walk all the way from the userNameDN entry back to the root in searching for the organizational configuration information. If this is done, the first configuration information that is found on the path from the userNameDN to the root should be used.

Once the object has been created, the configuration information can be retrieved using the accessor methods. This class is defined in Figure 9.1.

Notice that although the schema defines all of the attribute types as strings, only the accessor and mutator for the logoFileLocation fields use a

```
1. package userconfig;
2.
3. import netscape.ldap.util.*;
4. import java.util.*;
5. import netscape.ldap.*;
6.
7. public class CorporateClothing {
8.    private int shirtSize;
9.    private char shirtGender;
10.    private int jacketSize;
11.    private char jacketGender;
12.    private java.lang.String logoFileLocation;
13.    public LDAPConnection ld;
14.
15. public CorporateClothing() {
16.    super();
17. }
18.
19. public CorporateClothing(String userNameDN, LDAPConnection ld) {
20.      Enumeration myValues;
21.    // assume connection is already bound
22.    try {
23.      LDAPSearchResults myResults = ld.search(userNameDN,
24.        LDAPv2.SCOPE_BASE, "objectClass=*", null, false);
25.      LDAPEntry myEntry = myResults.next();
26.      LDAPAttributeSet entryAttrs = myEntry.getAttributeSet();
27.      LDAPAttribute myJacketGenderAttr =
28.        entryAttrs.getAttribute("jacketGender");
29.      myValues = myJacketGenderAttr.getStringValues();
30.      String myJacketGenderString = (String)
31.        myValues.nextElement(); // there should only be one
32.      jacketGender = myJacketGenderString.charAt(0);
33.      LDAPAttribute myJacketSizeAttr =
34.        entryAttrs.getAttribute("jacketSize");
35.      myValues = myJacketSizeAttr.getStringValues();
36.      String myJacketSizeString = (String)
37.        myValues.nextElement(); // there should only be one
38.      Integer myJacketSize = new Integer(myJacketSizeString);
39.      jacketSize = myJacketSize.intValue();
40.      LDAPAttribute myShirtGenderAttr =
41.        entryAttrs.getAttribute("shirtGender");
42.      myValues = myShirtGenderAttr.getStringValues();
43.      String myShirtGenderString = (String)
44.        myValues.nextElement(); // there should only be one
45.      shirtGender = myShirtGenderString.charAt(0);
46.      LDAPAttribute myShirtSizeAttr =
47.        entryAttrs.getAttribute("shirtSize");
48.      myValues = myShirtSizeAttr.getStringValues();
```

Figure 9.1   *Listing for user configuration application*

```
49.       String myShirtSizeString = (String)
50.         myValues.nextElement(); // there should only be one
51.       Integer myShirtSize = new Integer(myJacketSizeString);
52.       shirtSize = myShirtSize.intValue();
53.    } catch (LDAPException e) {
54.       return;
55.    } catch (Exception e) {
56.       return;
57.    }
58.    // now get the logo file location from the parent org
59.    try {
60.      DN myDN = new DN(userNameDN);
61.      DN parentDN = myDN.getParent();
62.      LDAPSearchResults myResults =
63.        ld.search(parentDN.toRFCString(), LDAPv2.SCOPE_BASE,
64.        "objectClass=*", null, false);
65.      LDAPEntry myEntry = myResults.next();
66.      LDAPAttributeSet entryAttrs = myEntry.getAttributeSet();
67.      LDAPAttribute myLogoFileAttr =
68.        entryAttrs.getAttribute("logoFileLocation");
69.      myValues = myLogoFileAttr.getStringValues();
70.      logoFileLocation = (String) myValues.nextElement();
71.    } catch (LDAPException e) {
72.      return;
73.    } catch (Exception e) {
74.      return;
75.    }
76. }
77.
78. public void getConfigFromLDAP(String userNameDN) throws
79.    LDAPException {
80.      Enumeration myValues;
81.    // assume connection is already bound
82.    try {
83.      LDAPSearchResults myResults = ld.search(userNameDN,
84.        LDAPv2.SCOPE_BASE, "objectClass=*", null, false);
85.      LDAPEntry myEntry = myResults.next();
86.      LDAPAttributeSet entryAttrs =
87.        myEntry.getAttributeSet();
88.      LDAPAttribute myJacketGenderAttr =
89.        entryAttrs.getAttribute("jacketGender");
90.      myValues = myJacketGenderAttr.getStringValues();
91.      String myJacketGenderString = (String)
92.        myValues.nextElement(); // there should only be one
93.      jacketGender = myJacketGenderString.charAt(0);
94.      LDAPAttribute myJacketSizeAttr =
95.        entryAttrs.getAttribute("jacketSize");
96.      myValues = myJacketSizeAttr.getStringValues();
```

Figure 9.1   *Listing for user configuration application (continued)*

```
97.      String myJacketSizeString = (String)
98.        myValues.nextElement(); // there should only be one
99.      Integer myJacketSize = new Integer(myJacketSizeString);
100.      jacketSize = myJacketSize.intValue();
101.    LDAPAttribute myShirtGenderAttr =
102.      entryAttrs.getAttribute("shirtGender");
103.    myValues = myShirtGenderAttr.getStringValues();
104.    String myShirtGenderString = (String)
105.      myValues.nextElement(); // there should only be one
106.    shirtGender = myShirtGenderString.charAt(0);
107.    LDAPAttribute myShirtSizeAttr =
108.      entryAttrs.getAttribute("shirtSize");
109.    myValues = myShirtSizeAttr.getStringValues();
110.    String myShirtSizeString = (String)
111.      myValues.nextElement(); // there should only be one
112.    Integer myShirtSize = new Integer(myJacketSizeString);
113.    shirtSize = myShirtSize.intValue();
114.  } catch (LDAPException e) {
115.    return;
116.  } catch (Exception e) {
117.    return;
118.  }
119.  // now get the logo file location from the parent org
120.  try {
121.    DN myDN = new DN(userNameDN);
122.    DN parentDN = myDN.getParent();
123.    LDAPSearchResults myResults =
124.      ld.search(parentDN.toRFCString(),
125.      LDAPv2.SCOPE_BASE, "objectClass=*", null, false);
126.    LDAPEntry myEntry = myResults.next();
127.    LDAPAttributeSet entryAttrs =
128.      myEntry.getAttributeSet();
129.    LDAPAttribute myLogoFileAttr =
130.      entryAttrs.getAttribute("logoFileLocation");
131.    myValues = myLogoFileAttr.getStringValues();
132.    logoFileLocation = (String) myValues.nextElement();
133.  } catch (LDAPException e) {
134.    return;
135.  } catch (Exception e) {
136.    return;
137.  }
138. }
139.
140. public char getJacketGender() {
141.   return jacketGender;
142. }
143.
144. public int getJacketSize() {
```

Figure 9.1 *Listing for user configuration application (continued)*

```
145.    return jacketSize;
146. }
147.
148. public LDAPConnection getLd() {
149.    return ld;
150. }
151.
152. public java.lang.String getLogoFileLocation() {
153.    return logoFileLocation;
154. }
155.
156. public char getShirtGender() {
157.    return shirtGender;
158. }
159.
160. public int getShirtSize() {
161.    return shirtSize;
162. }
163.
164. public void setJacketGender(char newJacketGender) {
165.    jacketGender = newJacketGender;
166. }
167.
168. public void setJacketSize(int newJacketSize) {
169.    jacketSize = newJacketSize;
170. }
171.
172. public void setLd( LDAPConnection newLd) {
173.    ld = newLd;
174. }
175.
176. public void setLogoFileLocation(java.lang.String
177.    newLogoFileLocation) {
178.    logoFileLocation = newLogoFileLocation;
179. }
180.
181. public void setShirtGender(char newShirtGender) {
182.    shirtGender = newShirtGender;
183. }
184.
185. public void setShirtSize(int newShirtSize) {
186.    shirtSize = newShirtSize;
187. }
188.
189. public void storeConfigInLDAP(String userDN,
190.    CorporateClothing config) throws LDAPException {
191.
192.    LDAPModificationSet myChanges = new
```

Figure 9.1   *Listing for user configuration application (continued)*

```
193.       LDAPModificationSet();
194.    Character myJacketGender = new Character(jacketGender);
195.    String jacketGenderString = myJacketGender.toString();
196.    LDAPAttribute attrJacketGender = new
197.       LDAPAttribute( "jacketGender", jacketGenderString);
198.    myChanges.add( LDAPModification.REPLACE,
199.       attrJacketGender );
200.    Character myShirtGender = new Character(shirtGender);
201.    String shirtGenderString = myShirtGender.toString();
202.    LDAPAttribute attrShirtGender = new
203.       LDAPAttribute( "shirtGender", shirtGenderString);
204.    myChanges.add( LDAPModification.REPLACE,
205.       attrShirtGender );
206.    Integer myShirtSize = new Integer(shirtSize);
207.    String shirtSizeString = myShirtSize.toString();
208.    LDAPAttribute attrShirtSize = new
209.       LDAPAttribute( "shirtSize", shirtSizeString);
210.    myChanges.add( LDAPModification.REPLACE,
211.       attrShirtSize );
212.    Integer myJacketSize = new Integer(jacketSize);
213.    String jacketSizeString = myJacketSize.toString();
214.    LDAPAttribute attrJacketSize = new
215.       LDAPAttribute( "jacketSize", jacketSizeString);
216.    myChanges.add( LDAPModification.REPLACE,
217.       attrJacketSize );
218.    try {
219.       ld.modify(userDN, myChanges);
220.    } catch (LDAPException e) {
221.       return;
222.    }
223.  }
224. }
```

Figure 9.1   *Listing for user configuration application (continued)*

string. The size fields use int values, and the gender fields use char values. Notice that the constructor handles the conversion from the LDAP string value to the appropriate internal representation. Strings are more convenient for LDAP browsing and other simple tools often used for debugging to easily view attribute values.

The *storeConfigInLDAP* method handles changes that are to be made to the stored configuration information. Notice that this method takes a DN as an input parameter. This allows for easy copying of the configuration information from one user to another. Notice also that this method does not write the logoFileLocation back out to the Directory. This is a conscious choice that allows for user configuration information to be updated independently of the organizational configuration information.

Using LDAP to Store Application-Defined Access Control Information

In previous chapters, we showed how NDS and Active Directory maintain access control information. Unfortunately, this information can be used only to restrict access to information stored in the Directory. Most applications have needs beyond this. This section shows how LDAP can be used to meet these needs. Consider an electronic commerce application that maintains a store. This application allows users to purchase a wide variety of items from a Web site. In order to make this happen, the application also needs to allow users to create new items to be made available for sale. Additionally, the application needs to allow for different types of changes to be made to the items that are up for sale.

The LDAP group concept can be used to facilitate these access control features. An entry in the Directory is created for each item that is available for purchase in the store. Each of these "item entries" references a group entry in the Directory. These referenced group entries contain the access control information for the store. Membership in the group indicates that privileges have been granted. The use of groups is especially attractive in NDS and Active Directory because they maintain the integrity of groups of DNs. This means that if a user object is a member of a group, and that user is deleted from the Directory, the user is also removed from any groups in which he or she held membership. Furthermore, if a user-object's DN is changed (via the LDAP Modify DN operation), then the value in the group is updated with the new name of the user.

A different group can be created for each item to which access rights need to be granted. However, because each item contains a group reference, many items can reference the same group, and the item entries can share access control lists. Whenever a user tries to manipulate an item in the store, the electronic commerce application checks the appropriate group entry to see if that user has sufficient access rights. The item entries are represented using this object class:

```
( 1.3.6.1.4.1.5515.6.1.3 NAME 'itemEntry' SUP top
STRUCTURAL MUST (updatePermission $ deletePermission))
```

The attribute types for the entry are defined as

```
(1.3.6.1.4.1.5515.6.2.2 NAME 'updatePermission' SUP
distinguishedName )
```

```
(1.3.6.1.4.1.5515.6.2.3 NAME 'deletePermission' SUP
distinguishedName )
```

Notice that the OIDs for these object class definitions and attribute-type definitions continue in the sequence established for the previous example. The attribute types use DN syntax so that NDS and Active Directory can maintain the integrity of the access control lists. DNs are assumed to reference those entries in the Directory with the object class *groupOfNames*. These groupOf-Names entries need not be used exclusively for the access control lists of the on-line store. Note also that both Access Control Lists (ACLs) of an itemEntry could actually reference the same group. The most commonly used functions of the Access Control package will be those that are used to check access control. The package will also provide other functions for system maintenance. These main-tenance functions allow for updating the access control lists and adding new item entries to the Directory. These main workhorse functions are

- addPermissionToGroup. Adds a user as a member of the specified group. In effect, this function gives the user permission to perform the actions that are specified based on the references to this group.
- removePermissionFromGroup. Removes a user as a member of the speci-fied group. In effect, this function takes away the user permission to per-form the actions that are specified based on the references to this group.
- checkDeleteItemAccess. Determines if the specified user is a member of the group pointed to by the deletePermission group
- checkUpdateItemAccess. Determines if the specified user is a member of the group pointed to by the updatePermission group
- addItem. Creates a new item entry in the Directory

The class also maintains accessor and mutator functions for the following inaccessible fields:

- itemDN. DN of an item for which access is to be checked
- updatePermissionGroup. The DN of the group entry in the Directory which contains the ACL for users who are allowed to make changes to the item in the store
- deletePermissionGroup. The DN of the group entry in the Directory which contains the ACL for users who are allowed to make deletions to the item in the store
- ld. The LDAPConnection object which is used to initiate LDAP operations to the Directory

The class also has two constructors. The first constructor is for use in ma-nipulating existing entries in the Directory. It takes two parameters: a string that contains the DN of the itemEntry in the Directory and an LDAPConnection ob-ject that has already been bound to the LDAP server. The other constructor is used in creation of new itemEntry objects in the Directory. It simply takes an LDAPConnection object. The mutator methods are then called to update the fields as appropriate. Since both attribute types are specified as mandatory, both the updatePermissionGroup and the deletePermissionGroup mutators must be called. Once the fields have been set to appropriate values, the addItem method can be called. The code for the class is in Figure 9.2.

Notice that this class does not place the methods that initiate the LDAP op-erations inside of a try-catch clause. The methods simply allow any exceptions

```
1.  package accesscontrol;
2.
3.  import java.util.*;
4.  import netscape.ldap.*;
5.
6.  public class ItemEntry {
7.     private java.lang.String itemDN;
8.     private java.lang.String updatePermissionGroup;
9.     private String deletePermissionGroup;
10.    private netscape.ldap.LDAPConnection ld;
11.
12. public ItemEntry(String itemDN, LDAPConnection ld)
13.    throws LDAPException {
14.    super();
15.    this.ld = ld;
16.    this.itemDN = itemDN;
17.    String myFilter = "objectClass=*";
18.    LDAPSearchResults res =  ld.search( itemDN,
19.      LDAPv2.SCOPE_BASE, myFilter, null, false );
20.    LDAPEntry myEntry = (LDAPEntry) res.nextElement();
21.    LDAPAttributeSet myAttrs = myEntry.getAttributeSet();
22.    LDAPAttribute deletePermissionAttr =
23.      myAttrs.getAttribute("deletePermission");
24.    Enumeration myValues =
25.      deletePermissionAttr.getStringValues();
26.    deletePermissionGroup = (String) myValues.nextElement();
27.    LDAPAttribute updatePermissionAttr =
28.      myAttrs.getAttribute("updatePermission");
29.    myValues = updatePermissionAttr.getStringValues();
30.      updatePermissionGroup = (String) myValues.nextElement();
31. }
32.
33. public ItemEntry(LDAPConnection ld) {
34.    super();
35.    this.ld = ld;
36.    itemDN = null;
37.    deletePermissionGroup = null;
38.    updatePermissionGroup = null;
39. }
40.
41. public void addItem(String itemDN) throws LDAPException {
42.    LDAPAttributeSet attributes = new LDAPAttributeSet();
43.    LDAPAttribute myAttribute = new
44.    LDAPAttribute("updatePermission", updatePermissionGroup);
45.      attributes.add(myAttribute);
46.    myAttribute = new LDAPAttribute("deletePermission",
47.      deletePermissionGroup);
48.    attributes.add(myAttribute);
```

Figure 9.2   *Listing for application-defined access control*

```
49.    LDAPAttribute objectClassAttribute = new
50.      LDAPAttribute("objectClass");
51.    objectClassAttribute.addValue("top");
52.    objectClassAttribute.addValue("itemEntry");
53.    attributes.add(objectClassAttribute);
54.    LDAPEntry myEntry = new LDAPEntry(itemDN, attributes);
55.    // all required attributes have been successfully added
56.    ld.add(myEntry);
57.  }
58.
59.  public void addPermissionToGroup(String userDN,
60.    String groupDN) throws LDAPException {
61.    LDAPModificationSet myChanges = new LDAPModificationSet();
62.    LDAPAttribute newMember = new LDAPAttribute( "member",
63.      userDN);
64.    myChanges.add( LDAPModification.ADD, newMember );
65.    ld.modify(userDN, myChanges);
66.  }
67.
68.  public boolean checkDeleteItemAccess(String userDN)
69.    throws LDAPException {
70.    LDAPAttribute memberToCheck = new LDAPAttribute( "member",
71.      userDN);
72.    boolean retValue = ld.compare(deletePermissionGroup,
73.      memberToCheck);
74.    return retValue;
75.  }
76.
77.  public boolean checkUpdateItemAccess(String userDN)
78.    throws LDAPException {
79.    LDAPAttribute memberToCheck = new LDAPAttribute( "member",
80.      userDN);
81.    boolean retValue = ld.compare(updatePermissionGroup,
82.      memberToCheck);
83.    return retValue;
84.  }
85.
86.  public String getDeletePermissionGroup() {
87.    return deletePermissionGroup;
88.  }
89.
90.  public java.lang.String getItemDN() {
91.    return itemDN;
92.  }
93.
94.  public netscape.ldap.LDAPConnection getLd() {
95.    return ld;
96.  }
```

Figure 9.2   *Listing for application-defined access control (continued)*

```
97.
98. public java.lang.String getUpdatePermissionGroup() {
99.    return updatePermissionGroup;
100. }
101.
102. public void removePermissionFromGroup(String userDN,
103. String itemDN) throws LDAPException {
104.    LDAPModificationSet myChanges = new
105.      LDAPModificationSet();
106.    LDAPAttribute oldMember = new LDAPAttribute( "member",
107.      userDN);
108.    myChanges.add( LDAPModification.DELETE, oldMember );
109.    ld.modify(userDN, myChanges);
110. }
111.
112. public void setDeletePermissionGroup(String
113.    newDeletePermissionGroup) {
114.    deletePermissionGroup = newDeletePermissionGroup;
115. }
116.
117. public void setItemDN(java.lang.String newItemDN) {
118.    itemDN = newItemDN;
119. }
120.
121. public void setLd(netscape.ldap.LDAPConnection newLd) {
122.    ld = newLd;
123. }
124.
125. public void setUpdatePermissionGroup(String
126.    newUpdatePermissionGroup) {
127.    updatePermissionGroup = newUpdatePermissionGroup;
128. }
129. }
```

| Figure 9.2 | *Listing for application-defined access control (continued)* |

that are thrown to be returned to the calling routine. Since the ACL checking methods use the compare operation to determine group membership, this function does not allow for groups that contain other groups. Each ACL must contain individual user entries. This implementation might allow the groups to grow in such a way that their member attributes hold a large number of values. Since the group entries are never retrieved by this implementation, there should be no noticeable performance impact. Once an item is created in the Directory, it can then be added to the online store. A typical change to an item involves a change to the price. Before allowing the user to change the price of an item, the application creates an itemEntry object by passing in the DN of the item in the Directory. Then the application calls the checkUpdatePermission method. If this method returns true, then the user has permission and the price change operation can proceed. If the method returns false, then the user does not have permission and the price change operation should not proceed.

An LDAP-Enabled Mailing List Administration Application

One of the popular uses of the Internet is sending electronic mail (email). Various communities of users can easily communicate by making use of mailing lists. A mailing list represents a group of users that are interested in a common topic and holds the email address for each user in the group. A mailing list also has its own email address. When someone desires to send a message to the mailing list, it is addressed to the email address of the mailing list. Then the mailing list application redirects that message to each user's email address. This mailing list application must be able to respond to a variety of commands. One of the most popular mailing list applications in use is known as *Majordomo*. Majordomo operates by waiting for email to arrive at a particular address. The messages that it receives contain various commands that Majordomo is expected to carry out. The mailing list address is different than this command address. Commands that are sent to Majordomo do not result in messages being sent out to the entire mailing list. Majordomo attempts to execute the commands and returns the results of the commands to the originator of the command.

The most common commands that are available to users of Majordomo are specified below. Parameters to the commands are given in angle brackets ("<>").

- Subscribe <list>. Adds the sender of the command to the named mailing list
- Unsubscribe <list>. Removes the sender of the command from the named mailing list Digest <list>. A special form of subscribe. The sender of the command does not want to receive each message that is posted to the mailing list on an individual basis. The messages are batched up and sent to digest users on a periodic (normally daily) basis.[1]
- Index <list>. Returns a list of files that are available for the specified mailing list
- Get <list> <file>. Returns the specified file for the named mailing list to the sender of the command
- Who <list>. Returns a list of subscribers of the named mailing list to the sender of the command
- Which. Returns a list of mailing lists to which the sender of the command is subscribed
- Lists. Returns a list of the mailing lists that are managed by this Majordomo server

---

1. The digest command is an enhanced feature not found in all mailing list implementations.

This section will show how LDAP can be used in an implementation of a Majordomo mailing list application. In addition to defining schema elements as in the previous examples, this application will make use of a special DIT structure. When users subscribe to mailing lists they are added to the DIT, if they are not already in the DIT by virtue of a previous subscription. In a Majordomo application, the only piece of information about the user that we are guaranteed to know is the user's email address. Thus, other information about the user, such as given name and surname, that is mandatory in the NDS and Active Directory User object classes, must be optional in the object class to be used for this application. We will also define an object class for mailing list entries. Figure 9.3 shows an example of the proposed DIT for the mailing list applications.

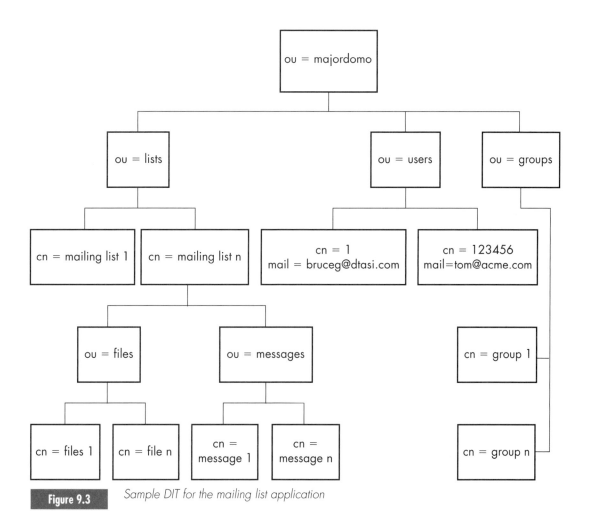

Figure 9.3 *Sample DIT for the mailing list application*

The ou entries in the above DIT are used for the purpose of organizing the DIT. They allow the files for a mailing list to be kept separately from the messages for the mailing list. The entries in the DIT that are named by cn are the specially designed entries for the application. The schema that is used for these entries is

```
( 1.3.6.1.4.1.5515.6.1.4 NAME 'mailingList' SUP top
STRUCTURAL MUST cn  MAY ( digestMembers $ regularMembers))
```

```
( 1.3.6.1.4.1.5515.6.1.5 NAME 'mailingListFile' SUP top
STRUCTURAL MUST  ( cn $ fileText ))
```

```
( 1.3.6.1.4.1.5515.6.1.6 NAME 'mailingListMessage' SUP top
STRUCTURAL MUST (cn $ mail $ messageText  ))
```

```
( 1.3.6.1.4.1.5515.6.1.7 NAME 'mailingListMember' SUP top
STRUCTURAL MUST ( cn $ mail))
```

The attribute types for the entry are defined as

```
(1.3.6.1.4.1.5515.6.2.4 NAME 'digestMembers' SUP
distinguishedName )
```

```
(1.3.6.1.4.1.5515.6.2.5 NAME 'regularMembers' SUP
distinguishedName )
```

```
(1.3.6.1.4.1.5515.6.2.6 NAME 'fileText' EQUALITY octet-
StringMatch
SYNTAX 1.3.6.1.4.1.1466.115.121.1.40)
```

```
(1.3.6.1.4.1.5515.6.2.6 NAME 'messageText' EQUALITY octet-
StringMatch
SYNTAX 1.3.6.1.4.1.1466.115.121.1.40)
```

The mailing list application creates unique cn values for each new message and subscribed user. The cn values for each mailing list's files are the file names that are used in the get and index commands described above. Each mailingList entry in the Directory maintains two lists of DNs. Each DN in the digestMembers attribute is assumed to be a digest subscriber to the mailing list. Similarly, each DN in the regularMembers attribute is assumed to be a regular subscriber to the mailing list, that is, one that receives each message individually.

The processing for the *subscribe* command is simple. Search the "ou= users" container for an entry with the potential subscriber's email address as the value of the mail attribute. If such an entry is found, simply add the DN for that entry as a value of the regularMembers attribute for the named mailing list. If no entry in the "ou=users" container is found, then a new mailingListMember entry, is created with the sender's email address as the value of the mail attribute. A new unique cn attribute value is created for this entry. Once the entry is created, the DN for this new entry is added as a value of the regularMembers attribute for the named mailing list. Processing the *digest* command is identical to processing the subscribe command, except that the DNs are added to the digestMembers attribute instead of the regularMembers attribute.

Processing the *unsubscribe* command is the reverse of the subscribe command. First the search for the mailingListMember in the "ou=users" is undertaken. If no entry is found, then the processing terminates with a failure, since there is no user to unsubscribe. If an entry is found, then the DN value for that entry is removed from the regularMembers attribute and the digestMembers attribute. Note that the entry may be present as a value in either attribute, both attributes, or neither attribute.

Processing the *index* command is very simple. The application simply does a single level search for all of the mailingListFile entries in the "ou=Files" container beneath the entry for the specified mailing list. Processing the *get* command is also very simple. The specified mailingListFile entry in the "ou=Files" container beneath the entry for the specified mailing list is retrieved. The value of the fileText attribute is returned to the sender of the message. Processing of the *who* command is a little more complex than it might seem. First, all values of both the regularMembers and digestMembers are retrieved. Then the mail attribute for each DN in either list is retrieved and returned to the sender of the message. For mailing lists with large numbers of members, this can be a cumbersome operation.

Processing of the *which* command is a little harder. Again, search the "ou=users" container for an entry with the potential subscriber's email address as the value of the mail attribute. If such an entry is found, then search the "ou=groups" container for a group entry with a member attribute that has a value equal to the DN of the mailingListMember entry that was previously found. Finally, using the groups that were found, search the "ou=lists" container for mailing lists that have a matching regularMembers or digestMembers attribute value. Any matching mailingList entries are returned to the sender of the command. Processing the *lists* command simply involves returning the cn values for all entries in the "ou=lists" container.

Whenever a message arrives at the mailing list email address, the Majordomo application sends it out to all members of the mailing lists and creates a new mailingListMessage entry in the "ou=messages" container for that mailing list. Additionally, the application should update the current digest of messages that is being kept for digest subscribers of the mailing list. Notice how the combination of the DIT structure and schema enhancements makes the processing of the Majordomo commands simple.

Figures 9.4 through 9.9 show the code for this example. It is made up of six separate classes. The base class *Majordomo* defines the system methods *lists()* and *which()*. It also defines static protected methods that can be accessed by the other classes in the application which extend this class. The application also includes classes corresponding to each of the LDAP object classes that are defined above. These classes are *MailingList, MailingListMember,*

```
1.  package majordomo;
2.
3.  import java.lang.*;
4.  import java.util.*;
5.  import netscape.ldap.*;
6.  import netscape.ldap.util.*;
7.
8.  public class Majordomo {
9.    protected static LDAPConnection ld;
10.   protected static String majordomoDN;
11.
12. public Majordomo() {
13.   super();
14. }
15.
16. public LDAPConnection getLd() {
17.   return ld;
18. }
19.
20. public static String getMajordomoDN() {
21.   return majordomoDN;
22. }
23.
24. public static MailingList[] lists() throws LDAPException {
25.   DN myMailingListDN = new DN(majordomoDN);
26.   RDN myRDN = new RDN("ou=lists");
27.   myMailingListDN.addRDN(myRDN);
28.   String myFilter = new String("objectClass=mailingList");
29.   String[] myAttrs = { "cn" };
30.   LDAPSearchResults res = ld.search(
31.     myMailingListDN.toRFCString(), LDAPv2.SCOPE_ONE,
32.     myFilter, myAttrs, false );
33.   int numberOfLists = res.getCount();
34.   MailingList[] myMailingLists = new
35.     MailingList[numberOfLists];
36.   int i = 0;
37.   while (res.hasMoreElements()) {
38.     LDAPEntry myEntry = (LDAPEntry) res.nextElement();
39.     LDAPAttribute cnAttr = myEntry.getAttribute("cn");
40.     Enumeration myValues = cnAttr.getStringValues();
41.     String myCn = (String) myValues.nextElement();
42.     myMailingLists[i] = new MailingList(myCn);
43.     i += 1;
44.   }
45.   return myMailingLists;
46. }
47.
48. public void setLd(netscape.ldap.LDAPConnection newLd) {
```

Figure 9.4 *Code for the Majordomo base class*

```
49.    ld = newLd;
50. }
51.
52. public static void setMajordomoDN(String newMajordomoDN) {
53.    majordomoDN = newMajordomoDN;
54. }
55.
56. public static MailingList[] which(String emailAddress)
57.    throws LDAPException {
58.    Vector mailingListsFound = new Vector();
59.    MailingListMember myMember = new
60.      MailingListMember(emailAddress);
61.    DN searchbaseDN = new DN(majordomoDN);
62.    RDN groupsRDN = new RDN("ou=groups");
63.    searchbaseDN.addRDN(groupsRDN);
64.    String myFilter = new String("member=" +
65.      myMember.getDn());
66.    String[] myAttrs = { "cn" };
67.    LDAPSearchResults res =  ld.search(
68.      searchbaseDN.toRFCString(), LDAPv2.SCOPE_ONE, myFilter,
69.      myAttrs, false );
70.    int numberOfGroups = res.getCount();
71.    if (numberOfGroups == 0) {
72.      return null;
73.    }
74.    // we have the groups, now find the corresponding mailing
75.    // lists
76.    while (res.hasMoreElements()) {
77.      LDAPEntry myEntry = (LDAPEntry) res.nextElement();
78.      searchbaseDN = new DN(majordomoDN);
79.      RDN listsRDN = new RDN("ou=lists");
80.      searchbaseDN.addRDN(listsRDN);
81.      myFilter = new String("digestMembers=" +
82.        myEntry.getDN());
83.      LDAPSearchResults digestResults  =  ld.search(
84.        searchbaseDN.toRFCString(), LDAPv2.SCOPE_ONE,
85.        myFilter, myAttrs, false );
86.      while (digestResults.hasMoreElements()) {
87.        LDAPEntry mailingListEntry = (LDAPEntry)
88.          digestResults.nextElement();
89.        LDAPAttribute myCnAttribute =
90.          mailingListEntry.getAttribute("cn");
91.        String[] myMailingListNames =
92.          myCnAttribute.getStringValueArray();
93.        MailingList myMailingList = new
94.          MailingList(myMailingListNames[0]);
95.        mailingListsFound.addElement(myMailingList);
96.      }
```

Figure 9.4   *Code for the Majordomo base class (continued)*

```
97.      myFilter = new String("regularMembers=" +
98.        myEntry.getDN());
99.      LDAPSearchResults regularResults =  ld.search(
100.     searchbaseDN.toRFCString(), LDAPv2.SCOPE_ONE,
101.     myFilter, myAttrs, false );
102.   while (regularResults.hasMoreElements()) {
103.     LDAPEntry mailingListEntry = (LDAPEntry)
104.       regularResults.nextElement();
105.     LDAPAttribute myCnAttribute =
106.       mailingListEntry.getAttribute("cn");
107.     String[] myMailingListNames =
108.       myCnAttribute.getStringValueArray();
109.     MailingList myMailingList = new
110.       MailingList(myMailingListNames[0]);
111.     mailingListsFound.addElement(myMailingList);
112.   }
113.   }
114.   // the mailingListsFound Vector has all of the mailing
115.   // lists, now turn it into an array
116.   MailingList[] myMailingLists = new
117.     MailingList[mailingListsFound.size()];
118.   for (int i = 0; i < mailingListsFound.size(); i++) {
119.     myMailingLists[i] = (MailingList)
120.       mailingListsFound.elementAt(i);
121.   }
122.   return myMailingLists;
123. }
124. }
```

Figure 9.4   *Code for the Majordomo base class (continued)*

```
1. package majordomo;
2.
3. import java.lang.*;
4. import java.util.*;
5. import netscape.ldap.util.*;
6. import netscape.ldap.*;
7.
8. public class MailingList extends Majordomo {
9.   private String digestMembers;
10.    private String regularMembers;
11.    private String mailingListDN;
12.
13. public MailingList() {
14.    super();
15. }
16.
```

Figure 9.5   *Code for the MailingList class*

```
17. public MailingList(String mailingListName) throws LDAPException {
18.   super();
19.   DN myMailingListDN = new DN(this.majordomoDN);
20.   RDN myRDN = new RDN("ou=lists");
21.   myMailingListDN.addRDN(myRDN);
22.   myRDN = new RDN("cn=" + mailingListName);
23.   myMailingListDN.addRDN(myRDN);
24.   mailingListDN = myMailingListDN.toRFCString();
25.   String myFilter = new String("objectClass=*");
26.     LDAPSearchResults res =  ld.search( mailingListDN, LDAPv2.SCOPE_
      BASE, myFilter, null, false );
27.     LDAPEntry myEntry = (LDAPEntry) res.nextElement();
28.     LDAPAttributeSet myAttrs = myEntry.getAttributeSet();
29.     LDAPAttribute digestMembersAttr = myAttrs.getAttribute("digest-
      Members");
30.     Enumeration myValues = digestMembersAttr.getStringValues();
31.     digestMembers = (String) myValues.nextElement();
32.     LDAPAttribute regularMembersAttr = myAttrs.getAttribute
      ("regularMembers");
33.     myValues = regularMembersAttr.getStringValues();
34.     regularMembers = (String) myValues.nextElement();
35. }
36.
37. public void addDigestSubscriber(String emailAddress) throws LDAP-
    Exception {
38.   MailingListMember myMember;
39.   try {
40.     myMember = new MailingListMember(emailAddress);
41.   } catch (LDAPException e) {
42.       myMember = new MailingListMember();
43.       myMember.addMember();
44.   }
45.     LDAPModificationSet myChanges = new LDAPModificationSet();
46.     LDAPAttribute newMember = new LDAPAttribute( "member", myMember
      .getDn());
47.     myChanges.add( LDAPModification.ADD, newMember );
48.     ld.modify(digestMembers, myChanges);
49. }
50.
51. public void addRegularSubscriber(String emailAddress) throws LDAP-
    Exception {
52.   MailingListMember myMember;
53.   try {
54.     myMember = new MailingListMember(emailAddress);
55.   } catch (LDAPException e) {
56.       myMember = new MailingListMember();
57.       myMember.addMember();
58.   }
```

Figure 9.5   *Code for the MailingList class (continued)*

```
59.       LDAPModificationSet myChanges = new LDAPModificationSet();
60.       LDAPAttribute newMember = new LDAPAttribute( "member", myMember
          .getDn());
61.       myChanges.add( LDAPModification.ADD, newMember );
62.       ld.modify(regularMembers, myChanges);
63. }
64.
65. public java.lang.String getDigestMembers() {
66.    return digestMembers;
67. }
68.
69. public MailingListFile getFile(String fileName) throws netscape.ldap
    .LDAPException {
70.    DN searchbaseDN = new DN(mailingListDN);
71.    RDN filesRDN = new RDN("ou=files");
72.    RDN myFileRDN = new RDN("cn=" + fileName);
73.    searchbaseDN.addRDN(filesRDN);
74.    searchbaseDN.addRDN(myFileRDN);
75.    MailingListFile myFile = new MailingListFile(searchbaseDN.toRFC-
       String());
76.    return myFile;
77. }
78.
79. public String getMailingListDN() {
80.    return mailingListDN;
81. }
82.
83. public String getRegularMembers() {
84.    return regularMembers;
85. }
86.
87. public MailingListFile[] index() throws netscape.ldap.LDAP
    Exception {
88.    DN searchbaseDN = new DN(mailingListDN);
89.    RDN filesRDN = new RDN("ou=files");
90.    searchbaseDN.addRDN(filesRDN);
91.    String myFilter = new String("objectClass=mailingListFile");
92.    String[] myAttrs = { "cn" };
93.       LDAPSearchResults res =  ld.search( searchbaseDN.toRFCString(),
          LDAPv2.SCOPE_ONE, myFilter, myAttrs, false );
94.    int numberOfFiles = res.getCount();
95.    if (numberOfFiles == 0) {
96.     return null;
97.    }
98.    MailingListFile[] myFiles = new MailingListFile[numberOfFiles];
99.    int i = 0;
100.    while (res.hasMoreElements()) {
```

Figure 9.5   *Code for the MailingList class (continued)*

```
101.        LDAPEntry myEntry = (LDAPEntry) res.nextElement();
102.        String dn = myEntry.getDN();
103.        myFiles[i] = new MailingListFile(dn);
104.        i += 1;
105.      }
106.    return myFiles;
107. }
108.
109. public void removeDigestSubscriber(String emailAddress) throws
     netscape.ldap.LDAPException {
110.    MailingListMember myMember;
111.    try {
112.      myMember = new MailingListMember(emailAddress);
113.    } catch (LDAPException e) {
114.        myMember = new MailingListMember();
115.        myMember.addMember();
116.    }
117.      LDAPModificationSet myChanges = new LDAPModificationSet();
118.      LDAPAttribute newMember = new LDAPAttribute( "member", myMember
        .getDn());
119.      myChanges.add( LDAPModification.DELETE, newMember );
120.      ld.modify(digestMembers, myChanges);
121. }
122.
123. public void removeRegularSubscriber(String emailAddress) throws
     LDAPException {
124.    MailingListMember myMember;
125.    try {
126.      myMember = new MailingListMember(emailAddress);
127.    } catch (LDAPException e) {
128.        myMember = new MailingListMember();
129.        myMember.addMember();
130.    }
131.      LDAPModificationSet myChanges = new LDAPModificationSet();
132.      LDAPAttribute newMember = new LDAPAttribute( "member", myMember
        .getDn());
133.      myChanges.add( LDAPModification.DELETE, newMember );
134.      ld.modify(regularMembers, myChanges);
135. }
136.
137. public void setDigestMembers(String newDigestMembers) {
138.    digestMembers = newDigestMembers;
139. }
140.
141. public void setMailingListDN(String newMailingListDN) {
142.    mailingListDN = newMailingListDN;
143. }
```

Figure 9.5   *Code for the MailingList class (continued)*

```
144.
145. public void setRegularMembers(String newRegularMembers) {
146.    regularMembers = newRegularMembers;
147. }
148.
149. public MailingListMember[] who() throws netscape.ldap.LDAP-
     Exception {
150.    String myFilter = "objectClass=*";
151.    LDAPSearchResults regularMembersResults = ld.search( regular-
        Members, LDAPv2.SCOPE_BASE, myFilter, null, false );
152.    LDAPSearchResults digestMembersResults = ld.search( regular-
        Members, LDAPv2.SCOPE_BASE, myFilter, null, false );
153.    int numberOfMembers = regularMembersResults.getCount() +
        digestMembersResults.getCount();
154.    MailingListMember[] myMembers = new MailingListMember[number-
        OfMembers];
155.    int i = 0;
156.    while (regularMembersResults.hasMoreElements()) {
157.      LDAPEntry myEntry = (LDAPEntry) regularMembersResults.next-
          Element();
158.      LDAPAttributeSet myAttributes = myEntry.getAttributeSet();
159.      LDAPAttribute myEmailAddressAttr = myAttributes.getAttribute
          ("mail");
160.      String[] myEmailAddressValues = myEmailAddressAttr.get-
          StringValueArray();
161.      String dn = myEntry.getDN();
162.      myMembers[i] = new MailingListMember();
163.      myMembers[i].setDn(dn);
164.      myMembers[i].setEmailAddress(myEmailAddressValues[0]);
165.      i += 1;
166.    }
167.    while (digestMembersResults.hasMoreElements()) {
168.      LDAPEntry myEntry = (LDAPEntry) digestMembersResults.next-
          Element();
169.      LDAPAttributeSet myAttributes = myEntry.getAttributeSet();
170.      LDAPAttribute myEmailAddressAttr = myAttributes.getAttribute
          ("mail");
171.      String[] myEmailAddressValues = myEmailAddressAttr.get-
          StringValueArray();
172.      String dn = myEntry.getDN();
173.      myMembers[i] = new MailingListMember();
174.      myMembers[i].setDn(dn);
175.      myMembers[i].setEmailAddress(myEmailAddressValues[0]);
176.      i += 1;
177.    }
178.    return myMembers;
179. }
180. }
```

Figure 9.5   *Code for the MailingList class (continued)*

```
1. package majordomo;
2.
3. import netscape.ldap.*;
4.
5. public class MailingListFile extends Majordomo {
6.     private String dn;
7.     private byte[] fileContents;
8.
9. public MailingListFile() {
10.    super();
11. }
12.
13. public MailingListFile(String fileNameDN) throws LDAPException {
14.    String myFilter = "objectClass=mailingListFile";
15.      LDAPSearchResults res =  ld.search( fileNameDN,
   LDAPv2.SCOPE_BASE, myFilter, null, false );
16.      LDAPEntry myEntry = (LDAPEntry) res.nextElement();
17.      dn = myEntry.getDN();
18.      LDAPAttributeSet myAttributes = myEntry.getAttributeSet();
19.      LDAPAttribute myContents =
   myAttributes.getAttribute("fileText");
20.      byte[][] myContentsArray = myContents.getByteValueArray();
21.      fileContents = myContentsArray[0];
22. }
23.
24. public String getDn() {
25.    return dn;
26. }
27.
28. public byte[] getFileContents() {
29.    return fileContents;
30. }
31.
32. public void setDn(String newDn) {
33.    dn = newDn;
34. }
35.
36. public void setFileContents(byte[] newFileContents) {
37.    fileContents = newFileContents;
38. }
39. }
```

Figure 9.6   *Code for the MailingListFile class*

```
1. package majordomo;
2.
3. import netscape.ldap.util.*;
4. import netscape.ldap.*;
5. import java.util.*;
6.
7. public class MailingListMember extends Majordomo {
8.     private java.lang.String emailAddress;
9.     private java.lang.String dn;
10.
11. public MailingListMember() {
12.    super();
13. }
14.
15. public MailingListMember(String emailAddress) throws netscape.ldap
    .LDAPException {
16.    String myFilter = "mail=" + emailAddress;
17.     LDAPSearchResults res = ld.search(majordomoDN, LDAPv2.SCOPE_
        SUB, myFilter, null, false );
18.     LDAPEntry myEntry = (LDAPEntry) res.nextElement();
19.     dn = myEntry.getDN();
20.     this.emailAddress = emailAddress;
21. }
22.
23. public void addMember() throws netscape.ldap.LDAPException {
24.    BookCalendar myCalendar = new BookCalendar();
25.    Long myLong = new Long(myCalendar.getTimeAsLong());
26.    String myCn = new String(myLong.toString());
27.     LDAPAttributeSet attributes = new LDAPAttributeSet();
28.     LDAPAttribute myAttribute = new LDAPAttribute("cn", myCn);
29.     attributes.add(myAttribute);
30.     myAttribute = new LDAPAttribute("mail", emailAddress);
31.     attributes.add(myAttribute);
32.     LDAPAttribute objectClassAttribute = new LDAPAttribute("object-
        Class");
33.     objectClassAttribute.addValue("top");
34.     objectClassAttribute.addValue("mailingListMember");
35.     attributes.add(objectClassAttribute);
36.     DN entryDN = new DN(majordomoDN);
37.     RDN usersOU = new RDN("ou=users");
38.     entryDN.addRDN(usersOU);
39.     RDN memberRDN = new RDN("cn=" + myCn);
40.     entryDN.addRDN(memberRDN);
41.     LDAPEntry myEntry = new LDAPEntry(entryDN.toRFCString(),
        attributes);
42.    // all required attributes have been successfully added
43.     ld.add(myEntry);
44. }
45.
```

Figure 9.7   *Code for the MailingListMember class*

```
46. public java.lang.String getDn() {
47.    return dn;
48. }
49.
50. public java.lang.String getEmailAddress() {
51.    return emailAddress;
52. }
53.
54. public void setDn(java.lang.String newDn) {
55.    dn = newDn;
56. }
57.
58. public void setEmailAddress(java.lang.String newEmailAddress) {
59.    emailAddress = newEmailAddress;
60. }
61. }
```

Figure 9.7   *Code for the MailingListMember class (continued)*

```
1. package majordomo;
2.
3. import netscape.ldap.util.*;
4. import netscape.ldap.*;
5.
6. public class MailingListMessage extends Majordomo {
7.     private MailingListMember sender;
8.     private byte[] messageText;
9.     private java.lang.String dn;
10.
11. public MailingListMessage() {
12.    super();
13. }
14.
15. public void addMessageToList(MailingList mailingList) throws
    netscape.ldap.LDAPException {
16.    BookCalendar myCalendar = new BookCalendar();
17.    Long myLong = new Long(myCalendar.getTimeAsLong());
18.    String myCn = new String(myLong.toString());
19.     LDAPAttributeSet attributes = new LDAPAttributeSet();
20.     LDAPAttribute myAttribute = new LDAPAttribute("cn", myCn);
21.     attributes.add(myAttribute);
22.     myAttribute = new LDAPAttribute("mail", sender.getEmail-
        Address());
23.     attributes.add(myAttribute);
24.     myAttribute = new LDAPAttribute("messageText", messageText);
25.     LDAPAttribute objectClassAttribute = new LDAPAttribute("object-
        Class");
26.     objectClassAttribute.addValue("top");
27.     objectClassAttribute.addValue("mailingListMessage");
```

Figure 9.8   *Code for the MailingListMessage class*

```
28.      attributes.add(objectClassAttribute);
29.      DN entryDN = new DN(mailingList.getMailingListDN());
30.      RDN messagesOU = new RDN("ou=messages");
31.      entryDN.addRDN(messagesOU);
32.      RDN messageRDN = new RDN("cn=" + myCn);
33.      entryDN.addRDN(messageRDN);
34.      LDAPEntry myEntry = new LDAPEntry(entryDN.toRFCString(),
         attributes);
35.  // all required attributes have been successfully added
36.      ld.add(myEntry);
37. }
38.
39. public java.lang.String getDn() {
40.    return dn;
41. }
42.
43. public byte[] getMessageText() {
44.    return messageText;
45. }
46.
47. public MailingListMember getSender() {
48.    return sender;
49. }
50.
51. public void setDn(java.lang.String newDn) {
52.    dn = newDn;
53. }
54.
55. public void setMessageText(byte[] newMessageText) {
56.    messageText = newMessageText;
57. }
58.
59. public void setSender(MailingListMember newSender) {
60.    sender = newSender;
61. }
62. }
```

Figure 9.8   *Code for the MailingListMessage class (continued)*

```
1. package majordomo;
2.
3. public class BookCalendar
4.    extends java.util.GregorianCalendar {
5.
6. public long getTimeAsLong() {
7.    return time;
8. }
9. }
```

Figure 9.9   *Code for the BookCalendar class*

MailingListFile, and *MailingListMessage.* This is common in LDAP-enabled applications. Each object class is normally represented in the application with its own class. There is interaction among these classes that represents the actual relationship in the data model represented by the LDAP schema. The final class is a simple extension of the GregorianCalendar Java class, which allows us to get the current time as a long value, so that it can be used to synthesize cn attributes. Each of the five main classes includes, as usual, the accessor and mutator classes for the defined fields. Methods are defined in the classes in order to implement the Majordomo commands described in this section.

Installing LDAP-Enabled Applications

Whenever an LDAP-enabled application defines its own schema extensions, those extensions must be added to the LDAP server's schema. In LDAP, the subschemaSubentry operational attribute contains the Distinguished Name of the subschema entry (or subentry) that controls the schema for this entry. This operational attribute is available on each entry in the Directory and is supported by the latest versions of NDS and Active Directory. Using this DN and specifying a search filter of "objectClass=subschema," the schema for the LDAP server can be retrieved.

Although it is not specifically mentioned in RFC 2251, adding new object classes and attribute types can modify the schema specified in this entry.[2] To add a new attribute type to the schema, the modification type is specified as attributeType and the modification value must follow the attributeTypeDescription syntax as defined in RFC 2252. In addition, the attribute type description must have a 'SYNTAX' value, and the server must know this syntax. Otherwise the server will return an invalidAttributeSyntax error code (21). Neither NDS nor Active Directory allows for the definition of new attribute syntaxes. So, only the predefined set of syntaxes can be used to define new attribute types. Figure 9.10 shows, in LDIF format, an example modification that adds the messageText attribute defined above to the schema.

To add a new object class to the schema, the modification type is specified as objectClasses, and the modification value must follow the ObjectClassDescription syntax as defined in RFC 2252 [3]. If the object class contains mandatory or optional attributes, the server *must* refuse the modification if the attributes are not already defined in the subschema entry. Thus, the installation procedure must define any new attribute types prior to defining new object

---

2. The mechanisms for modifying the LDAP schema are described in the Internet Draft by Ludovic Poitou and Timothy Hahn, *LDAP Schema Update Procedures,* published July 18, 2001.

```
1. version: 1
2.     dn: cn=schema, dc=example, dc=com
3.     changetype: modify
4.     add: attributetypes
5.     attributetypes: (1.3.6.1.4.1.5515.6.2.6
6.     NAME 'messageText' EQUALITY octetStringMatch
7.     SYNTAX 1.3.6.1.4.1.1466.115.121.1.40)
```

Figure 9.10   *Modifying the schema subentry to add a new attribute type*

```
1. version: 1
2.     dn: cn=schema, dc=example, dc=com
3.     changetype: modify
4.     add: objectclasses
5.     objectclasses: ( 1.3.6.1.4.1.5515.6.1.7
6.     NAME 'mailingListMember' SUP top
7.     STRUCTURAL MUST ( cn $ mail))
```

Figure 9.11   *Modifying the schema subentry to add a new Object Class*

classes (see Figure 9.11).Other than modifying the schema, no other differences
are needed for an LDAP-enabled application. When modifying the schema of
NDS and Active Directory, administrative level privileges are required. This is
not normally the case for most general-purpose applications.

Limitations of LDAP

Several years ago, Tim Howes wrote an article describing his thoughts on what some appropriate uses were for LDAP.[1] As Howes is one of the inventors of LDAP, his thoughts should be seriously examined. His first step in describing the types of things that LDAP could be used to accomplish was to describe the types of things for which LDAP was inappropriate. To a certain extent, this book has taken the opposite approach. Up until now, we have only discussed how to build applications using LDAP. This chapter will discuss some of LDAP's limitations, and in certain situations, how these limitations can be overcome.

In his article, Howes classifies LDAP applications into three categories:

- Those that locate network users and resources
- Those that manage network users and resources
- Those that authenticate and secure network users and resources

The first class of applications is really just the White Pages application described in Chapter 2. The second class of applications is the set of standard network administration applications. To a certain extent the third class of applications represents the so-called *Single Sign-on* application. Historically, users have to sign on to multiple applications, each of which requires its own sign-on dialog. Each dialog may use a different user ID and password (or other authentication credentials). Additionally, network administrators are forced to maintain multiple user accounts within each of the applications. In a Single Sign-on system, the multiple authentication dialogs are replaced with a single dialog. The user has only to remember one user id and password combination. The network administrator needs only to maintain one set of user accounts. LDAP is widely used as the focal point of the user account management in the Single Sign-on application. In

---

1. Tim Howes, "LDAP: Use as Directed," *Data Communications,* February 7, 1999.

addition to Single Sign-on, this class of applications also uses the Directory to compute access control information.

Consider the three example applications that were discussed in Chapter 9. How do they fit in to the classification mentioned in Howes's article? Recall that the three applications are

- User and application configuration
- Application-defined permissions
- Mailing list application

These applications don't easily fit into the classification. User and application configuration is really an extension of the White Pages application. The application is simply storing more parameters that are known about the user in LDAP entries than were traditionally stored. The application-defined permissions application is really an extension of the authentication and security class of applications. Instead of using the native NDS or Active Directory access control mechanism, this application uses other LDAP features such as groups to define new permissions beyond those that are defined by the Directory service. The mailing list application falls into a different class of applications. This class is one that is still appropriate for use with LDAP. This class consists of

- Those applications that store data that is unlikely to change frequently but is accessed occasionally

This is a pretty generic description that will be refined as we go through some of the limitations of LDAP. Note that Howes's original classes fit this description as well. This new class is more of a "catchall" description than anything else. It is important to note that LDAP is not intended to replace relational databases in applications. It is likely that many applications currently use relational databases in such a way that the full capabilities of a relational database system are not used. The main capabilities of the relational database system that are missing from LDAP are the transaction processing capabilities. Going hand in hand with the transaction processing capabilities is the two-phase commit. In a two-phase commit system, data is not permanently written out to the database until the programmer explicitly *commits* the data. Thus, a programmer might create several new records in the database, then update several existing records, and finally delete several other existing records. If any of these numerous operations fails, then the programmer can easily back out all of the changes that were made. In this situation, once the programmer backs out the changes, the database is in the same state that it was in before any of these changes were made.

This two-phase commit feature is missing from LDAP. Consider the following scenario in which LDAP group entries are used. Each group in the Directory has a member attribute that may have many values. Each of the values of the member attribute is the DN of some other entry. Recall the user and application configuration application of Chapter 9. Assume that instead of using an

Auxiliary objects class to represent the configuration information a structural object class was used. In this scenario, there would be one configuration entry in the Directory for each user entry. Now, consider what happens when a user is deleted. In addition to the deletion of the user, the user's configuration entry should also be deleted. In NDS and Active Directory, whenever a user is removed from the Directory, all groups in which that user appeared as a value of the member attribute are updated. These groups are updated by removing the value corresponding to the user entry that has been deleted. So, if the user entry is deleted, and the system fails before the configuration entry is deleted, the system is in an inconsistent state. This results in "dangling" configuration entries for which no user entry exists. Furthermore, if the programmer decided to resolve the inconsistency by going back and adding the user, the system would not return to the state it was in prior to the deletion. This is because the Directory server would have removed that user from all groups in which he was a member. The programmer has no way to add the user back to those groups.

It is possible, albeit time consuming, to find the user configuration entries for which no corresponding user exists. In this situation, the programmer must write a dredging application that periodically searches the entire Directory for configuration entries for which no user entry exists. In a large Directory with millions of users, such a process is completely unworkable. There would be millions of configuration entries. For each configuration entry, the dredging process would issue a separate search to see if the corresponding user entry exists. Assuming that the LDAP server and the host on which it resides are reasonably stable, the user entry corresponding to the configuration entry would almost always exist. Thus, for the most part, the dredging process would be a big waste of time. But, there is no other way to determine if there are dangling configuration entries.

Thus, because of this limitation, LDAP should not be used in situations where there is heavy update usage. LDAP servers do not have the capability to recover to a consistent state in the face of failures. In these situations, a relational database system must be used.

LDAP is also not well suited to serve as a file system. While it is possible to store files in LDAP, as is done in the mailing list application, the messages that are stored in the Directory are accessed only as a whole piece. LDAP does not allow for the retrieval of part of an attribute. File systems allow for retrieval of files in a piecemeal fashion. The developer is allowed to specify a range of bytes, and the file system will return the portion of the file corresponding to the byte range. Related to this limitation is the one mentioned in Chapter 4, which we called the "Retrieval of Unwanted Data." Because LDAP allows for multiple values in a single attribute, and LDAP's search operation does not allow for the selective retrieval of attribute values, it is often the case that the LDAP application can end up retrieving many more attribute values than are necessary. Chapter 4 gives some guidance on working around this problem by making use of better schema and DIT structure designs.

Another feature that is present in relational database systems but missing in LDAP is the ability to do complex Join operations. A relational database join operation allows the result of a Select statement to be a combination of columns from several tables. Recall that in LDAP the result of a Search operation is a sequence of entries that have been retrieved from the Directory. In LDAP terminology, a Join would allow for the result of a Search to be a collection of "virtual" entries whose attributes were taken from several actual entries in the Directory. Because of the lack of a Join operation in LDAP, operations that could be executed in a single line of code in a relational database must be implemented as part of a loop when using LDAP. Consider the following scenario. Recall the application-defined permissions application from Chapter 9. How would we find out the applications to which users in a specified container have been granted access? In order to perform this operation, we would first have to search the container and retrieve all of the users in that container. Then, we would have to search for all of the access control entries that had each user. The code for this can get a little complex and is shown in Figure 10.1.

Notice that rather than being able to create a Join between the matching user entries and the matching item entries, the programmer must create two separate searches, one of which is nested inside the other. This scenario is similar to the implementation of the *which* operation in the mailing list application. In either case, the implementation will have much worse performance than the relational database Join. It is easy to imagine more complex scenarios that would require numerous nested search operations. The only way to work around these requirements in LDAP is to make use of more schema and DIT structure definitions. Thus, the complexity is embedded in the information in the Directory and not in the program.

What are some ways of working around these limitations? It is critical to understand that it is not always possible to work around these limitations. Thus, when the situation arises that LDAP is not an appropriate repository for an application's data, the programmer should accept LDAP's limitations and make use of a more appropriate repository. Many times, the techniques described in Chapter 4 can be used to place more intelligence in the schema and DIT structure designs and reduce the complexity of the application. These techniques should definitely be explored whenever possible. This is especially desirable when trying to avoid the problem of Retrieval of Unwanted Data.

In certain scenarios it is possible to work around the lack of two-phase commit in LDAP. This has been done in several cases by using a transaction monitor that creates a log in the Directory (or in a location in the file system) of each LDAP operation. Thus, prior to issuing a series of LDAP operations, each operation is first written to the application log. Once this is successful, the actual LDAP operations are submitted to the Directory. Thus, if the LDAP application is somehow interrupted, when the application is restarted, the first thing that it should do is to check the transaction log. The application can work backward

```
1. public ItemEntry[] findItemEntries(String containerName,
2.    String itemEntrySearchBase) throws LDAPException {
3.    // first get all of the users in the specified container
4.    String myFilter = new String("objectClass=person");
5.    String[] myAttrs = { "cn" };
6.    LDAPSearchResults res =  ld.search( containerName,
7.      LDAPv2.SCOPE_ONE, myFilter, myAttrs, false );
8.    int numberOfUsers = res.getCount();
9.    if (numberOfUsers == 0) {
10.     return null;
11.   }
12.   Vector myUserVector = new Vector();
13.   while (res.hasMoreElements()) {
14.     LDAPEntry myEntry = (LDAPEntry) res.nextElement();
15.     String myUserDN = myEntry.getDN();
16.     myUserVector.addElement(myUserDN);
17.   }
18.
19.   // we have found all of the users  . now find the corre-
20.   // sponding item entries
21.
22.   Vector myItemEntryVector = new Vector();
23.   for (int i=0; i < numberOfUsers; i++) {
24.      myFilter = new String("member=" +
25.       (String) myUserVector.elementAt(i));
26.      res =  ld.search( itemEntrySearchBase,
27.        LDAPv2.SCOPE_SUB, myFilter, myAttrs, false );
28.      while (res.hasMoreElements()) {
29.        LDAPEntry myEntry = (LDAPEntry) res.nextElement();
30.        String myItemEntryDN = myEntry.getDN();
31.        ItemEntry myItemEntry = new ItemEntry(myItemEntryDN,
32.          this.ld);
33.        myItemEntryVector.addElement(myItemEntry);
34.      }
35.    }
36.    ItemEntry[] myItemEntries = new
37.      ItemEntry[myItemEntryVector.size()];
38.    for (int i=0; i <  myItemEntryVector.size(); i++) {
39.       myItemEntries[i] = (ItemEntry)
40.         myItemEntryVector.elementAt(i);
41.    }
42.    return myItemEntries;
43. }
```

Figure 10.1 *Java code to find matching item entries for users in a specified container*

through the log to find out the last operation that was successful, and then pick up from that point and reissue any operations that had failed to be submitted. Finally, once the entire series of operations is successful, a marker is written to the transaction log. This marker is an indication of the successful completion of a series of LDAP operations.

Now, we can refine the definition of the types of applications for which LDAP is appropriate. In addition to the three original classifications, we have added a fourth. The complete updated list is

- Those that locate network users, resources, and user configuration information needed by the application
- Those that manage network users and resources
- Those that authenticate and secure network users and resources, and additionally provide security for application data and processes held outside of the Directory
- Those that store data that, once it has been added to the Directory, is unlikely to change frequently but is accessed occasionally, and the values need to be accessed only in their entirety, not on a byte-range basis

Remember that even in the above classification, if an application requires transactional integrity or has to do many "joins," then it may not be suitable as an LDAP application.

LDAP and XML

CHAPTER OBJECTIVES

XML is a relatively new means of representing structured information on the Internet, and it is ostensibly the successor to the HTML that is widely used in Web Browser–based applications today. This is the case even though many of the mechanisms used in XML are derived from earlier work on Standard Generalized Markup Language (SGML). XML is a specification of the World Wide Web consortium and is available from the W3C's Web site: *www.w3c.org/.* The second edition of Version 1.0 of XML is the latest version of XML available at the time this book was written. The current status of XML can be found at *www.w3.org/ XML/.* SGML is standard for defining descriptions of the structure of different types of electronic documents.

For our purposes, it makes just as much sense to consider XML to be a successor to the LDAP Data Interchange Format (LDIF) as defined in RFC 2849. LDIF defines a file format that is suitable for describing the entries that are held in a Directory. The LDIF format was originally developed and used in the University of Michigan LDAP implementation. The first use of LDIF was in describing Directory entries. Later, the format was expanded to allow representation of changes to Directory entries. The current recommendation for the use of XML in an LDAP environment is the Directory Services Markup Language (DSML). Just as LDIF does, DSML defines a file format that is suitable for describing LDAP entries. Both Novell and Microsoft have announced support for the DSML specification and are contributing to enhancements to the first version of the specification. DSML is the product of a consortium of vendors that have contributed

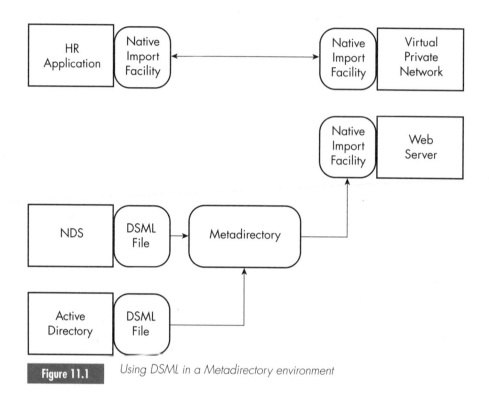

Figure 11.1   *Using DSML in a Metadirectory environment*

to the DSML standardization effort.[1] The Web site for the DSML consortium is www.dsml.org.

Why is it necessary to define a file format for LDAP? RFC 2849 provides an excellent explanation. There are a number of situations where a common interchange format is desirable. For example, one might wish to export a copy of the contents of a Directory server to a file, move that file to a different machine, and import the contents into a second Directory server. A well-defined format such as LDIF or DSML allows for integration with applications that want to have access to the Directory information but are not yet integrated with LDAP using the mechanisms described in Chapter 9. In these scenarios, an auxiliary application (often called a Metadirectory) can work behind the scenes to import data into the third-party application.

Note that Metadirectories can perform other actions in addition to data synchronization, but this is the most important one for our purpose. Both Microsoft and Novell produce Metadirectory offerings. Microsoft's is known as Microsoft Meta-Directory Service (MMS), and Novell's is Dir XML. The interaction of a Metadirectory with other Directory services is illustrated in Figure 11.1.

---

1. The founding partners of the consortium include Netscape, IBM, Novell, Microsoft, Sun Microsystems, Oracle, and Bowstreet.

Notice that the Metadirectory application uses the extracted information from NDS and Active Directory in a DSML format. Not all Metadirectories use DSML. They may use LDIF, for example. Additionally, by using a well-defined interchange format, development of data import tools from legacy systems is facilitated in other ways as well. Network administrators can perform many tasks using custom-written tasks rather than purchasing a Metadirectory product. A fairly simple set of tools written in awk or perl can, for example, convert a database of personnel information into an LDIF file. This file can then be imported into a Directory server, regardless of the internal database representation the target Directory server uses.

Before going into the discussion of DSML, we will first discuss the LDIF format. In its simplest form, an LDIF file is just a list of Directory entries. Each entry in the file begins with the DN of the entry, followed by all of the attribute-value pairs of the entry. If an attribute has multiple values, then the attribute name is repeated for each of the values. An LDIF file starts off with the version number of the LDIF format being used in the file. Until the LDIF specification is enhanced, the version number will always be the number 1. Figure 11.2 shows a typical LDIF file.

```
version: 1
dn: cn=Bruce Greenblatt, ou=Engineering, dc=dtasi, dc=com
objectclass: top
objectclass: person
objectclass: organizationalPerson
objectclass: inetOrgPerson
cn: Bruce Greenblatt
cn: Bruce G Greenblatt
givenName: Bruce
sn: Greenblatt
uid: bgreenblatt
telephonenumber: +1 408 555 1212
description: An LDAP Author.
mail: bgreenblatt@dtasi.com

dn: cn=Barney Fife, ou=Security, dc=dtasi, dc=com
objectclass: top
objectclass: person
objectclass: organizationalPerson
objectclass: inetOrgPerson
cn: Barney Fife
sn: Fife
uid: bfife
description: Deputy Sheriff
mail: bfife@dtasi.com
```

Figure 11.2   *Example LDIF file*

Notice how LDIF provides a straightforward translation of the Directory entry into a textual format. Each record in the LDIF file begins with the "dn" attribute definition. Each record in the LDIF file defines a single entry in the DIT. In addition to the ASCII text values in the attributes of the above example, LDIF also provides capabilities for indicating values as binary and non-ASCII text. In addition to providing an easy transformation of the DIT into a file, LDIF also defines a one-to-one correlation between LDAP operations that modify the DIT (e.g., add, delete, and modify) and a set of LDIF change records. Thus, there are two types of records in an LDIF file. One record type defines an entry in the DIT, and the other type defines a change to an entry in the DIT. The format of the LDIF change records is not important to the XML discussion and is omitted here.

A Quick XML Overview

XML is a markup specification language (just as HTML is a markup language) with which you can design ways of describing information (text or data). Once the data has been described using XML, it can be stored, transmitted, or processed by a program. Notice the similarity between the goals defined for LDIF and the goals of XML. XML doesn't say anything about what you should do with the data (although the choice of element names may hint at what they are for). The XML elements correspond to LDAP attributes. XML authors can create their own document types, which is exactly what the authors of DSML have done. XML document types are defined using a Document Type Definition (DTD). A DTD is a formal description of a particular type of document and defines what names are to be used for the different types of element, where they may occur, and how they all fit together. For example, Figure 11.3 shows what a DTD might contain if we wanted to create documents that described attributes, each of which contains several values.

This DTD defines an attribute as an element type containing zero or more values (denoted by the asterisk). Then the DTD goes on to define values as element types containing just plain text (Parsed Character Data or PCDATA). PCDATA values are "parsed" to remove special characters. If special characters are allowed to appear in the text, then the CDATA type is to be used instead. Validating parsers read the DTD before they read your document so that they can identify where every element type ought to come and how each relates to the other, so that applications which need to know this in advance (most editors, search engines, navigators, databases) can set themselves up correctly.

```
<!ELEMENT Attribute (Value)*>
<!ELEMENT Value (#PCDATA)>
```

Figure 11.3   *Example DTD*

```
<Attribute>
<Value>Bruce</Value>
<Value>Barney</Value>
<Value>Fred</Value>
</Attribute>
```

Figure 11.4   *Example XML document*

DTDs are defined using the XML Declaration Syntax. In this syntax, keywords begin with "<!" instead of just "<" as in a normal XML or HTML tag. Figure 11.4 shows an example of the attributes you can create.

Notice the similarity between an XML document and an HTML document. The XML tags correspond to HTML tags. In XML all tags must have a corresponding end tag. The DTD for DSML is a slightly more complex version of the example in Figure 11.3. An XML document consists of entities. Each XML entity consists of one or more elements, which in turn consist of one or more attributes. The different kind of entities, elements, and attributes that can be present in the document are defined in the document's DTD.

DSML

Since an XML document consists of the components described above, in a DSML document, the entities, elements, and attributes that are available are defined in the DSML DTD. A DSML document can describe either LDAP entries or an LDAP schema.[2] We will worry only about the portion that describes LDAP entries. Figure 11.5 shows the important components of the DSML DTD.

The line in the DTD

```
<!ELEMENT dsml (directory-schema?,directory-entries?)>
```

indicates that a DSML document is either a schema or some LDAP entries. The question mark indicates that the specified XML element is optional. The line in the DTD

```
<!ELEMENT directory-entries (entry*)>
```

indicates that the Directory entries element is actually composed of zero or more entry elements. The asterisk indicates that the specified XML element can be repeated any number of times. So, in a DSML document, there can be as many entry elements as needed to represent the LDAP entries in the DIT. The line in the DTD

---

2. Future versions of DSML will also allow for LDAP operations to be included. This feature is not part of DSML 1.0.

```
<!ELEMENT dsml (directory-schema?,directory-entries?)>

<!ELEMENT directory-entries (entry*)>

<!ELEMENT entry (objectclass*,attr*)>

<!ATTLIST entry
  dn  %distinguished-name;  #REQUIRED
>

<!ELEMENT objectclass (oc-value+)>
<!ATTLIST objectclass
  ref    %uri-ref; #IMPLIED
>

<!ELEMENT oc-value (#PCDATA)>
<!ATTLIST oc-value
  ref    %uri-ref; #IMPLIED
>

<!ELEMENT attr (value+)>
<!ATTLIST attr
  name  CDATA      #REQUIRED
  ref    %uri-ref; #IMPLIED
>

<!ELEMENT value (#PCDATA)>
<!ATTLIST value
  encoding CDATA "base64"
>
```

Figure 11.5	*DSML DTD for LDAP entries*

```
<!ELEMENT entry (objectclass*,attr*)>
```

indicates that each entry element consists of zero or more objectClass elements followed by zero or more attr elements. DSML calls out the objectClass attribute of the LDAP entry for special treatment. Notice that the DSML document can represent an LDAP entry without any objectClass values, or it can represent an LDAP entry with only objectClass values. Neither of these types of entries is allowed to occur in an LDAP DIT. The top object class has only the objectClass attribute type, but it is an abstract object class and thus entries of the top object class cannot be created in the DIT. The lines in the DTD

```
<!ATTLIST entry
  dn  %distinguished-name;  #REQUIRED
>
```

indicate a feature of the DTD syntax that we haven't discussed. In addition to being composed of child elements, the "!ATTLIST" tag in the DTD indicates that the entry element has an additional attribute called the dn. Of course, the dn attribute of an entry holds the DN of the entry. Notice the "=REQUIRED" keyword. This means that the specified XML attribute must be present in the entry. According to the DSML specification, the DTD developers decided to express the distinguished name as an XML attribute rather than as a child element because it uniquely identifies the entry. The lines in the DTD

```
<!ELEMENT objectclass (oc-value+)>
<!ATTLIST objectclass
   ref    %uri-ref; #IMPLIED
>
```

indicate that an objectclass element consists of one or more oc-value elements. Thus a plus sign is similar to the asterisk in XML, except that when the plus sign is used, at least one of the specified elements must occur in the document. The objectClass element also has an optional ref element. An objectClass's ref is a URI Reference to an attribute-type defining the objectClass's Directory attribute and is not normally used. The "=IMPLIED" keyword means that the specified attribute can be omitted and that there is no default value. The rest of the lines in the DTD are similar:

```
<!ELEMENT oc-value (#PCDATA)>
<!ATTLIST oc-value
   ref    %uri-ref; #IMPLIED
>
```

and indicate that the oc-value elements are composed of Parsed Character Data (PCDATA) just as in the original example DTD in Figure 11.3. The DTD also has the optional ref attribute. These lines in the DTD

```
<!ELEMENT attr (value+)>
<!ATTLIST attr
   name  CDATA      #REQUIRED
   ref    %uri-ref; #IMPLIED
>
```

indicate that an attr element is composed of one or more value elements. Each attr element has a required attribute called name, which gives the name of the attribute type for the entry. It also has the optional ref attribute. These lines in the DTD

```
<!ELEMENT value (#PCDATA)>
<!ATTLIST value
   encoding CDATA "base64"
>
```

indicate that each value element is simply PCDATA. It has an attribute encoding, which indicates if base64 encoding has been used for binary data. For the encoding attribute, neither the =REQUIRED specifier nor the =IMPLIED specifier is used. This means that when the encoding attribute is present then only the

```
<dsml:dsml xmlns:dsml="http://www.dsml.org/DSML">
  <!- a document with only directory entries ->
  <dsml:directory-entries>
    <dsml:entry dn="...">...</dsml:entry>
    <dsml:entry dn="...">...</dsml:entry>
    <dsml:entry dn="...">...</dsml:entry>
    ...
  </dsml:directory-entries>
</dsml:dsml>
```

Figure 11.6   *Structure of a typical DSML document*

```
<dsml:dsml xmlns:dsml="http://www.dsml.org/DSML">
<dsml:directory-entries>
<dsml:entry dn="cn=Bruce Greenblatt,
 ou=Engineering, dc=dtasi, dc=com ">
  <dsml:objectclass>
    <dsml:oc-value>top</dsml:oc-value>
    <dsml:oc-value>person</dsml:oc value>
    <dsml:oc-value>organizationalPerson</dsml:oc-value>
    <dsml:oc-value>inetOrgPerson</dsml:oc-value>
  </dsml:objectclass>
  <dsml:attr name="cn">
    <dsml:value>Bruce Greenblatt</dsml:value>
    <dsml:value>Bruce G Greenblatt</dsml:value>
  </dsml:attr>
  <dsml:attr name="givenname">
    <dsml:value>Bruce</dsml:value>
  </dsml:attr>
  <dsml:attr name="sn">
    <dsml:value>Greenblatt</dsml:value>
  </dsml:attr>
  <dsml:attr name="uid">
    <dsml:value>bgreenblatt</dsml:value>
  </dsml:attr>
  <dsml:attr name="telephonenumber">
    <dsml:value>+1 408 555 1212</dsml:value>
  </dsml:attr>
  <dsml:attr name="description">
    <dsml:value>An LDAP Author</dsml:value>
  </dsml:attr>
  <dsml:attr name="mail">
    <dsml:value>bgreenblatt@dtasi.com</dsml:value>
  </dsml:attr>
</dsml:entry>
<dsml:entry dn="cn=Barney Fife, ou=Security,
 dc=dtasi, dc=com ">
```

Figure 11.7   *Example DSML file*

value "base64" is allowed. If other values were allowed, then they would be listed along with the "base64" value. The encoding attribute is used to identify LDAP attributes containing binary data. These LDAP attributes are encoded using an encoding scheme identified by the encoding on the value element. At present, DSML supports only base64 as a value, but the encoding XML attribute is included in order to enable support for other encoding schemes in the future. Base64 encoding is described in RFC 1521. There is no other encoding allowed in DSML documents.

The document element of DSML is of the type dsml, which may have a child element of the type Directory-entries. This element, in turn, has child elements of the type entry. Figure 11.6 shows the structure of a typical DSML document.

Notice that each DSML tag begins with the keyword "dsml" in order to identify it as such. In XML, this is known as the namespace. The use of the DSML namespace is specified on the first line in the listing in Figure 11.7. The XML's keyword specifies the use of the namespace indicated by the following identifier. Each tag has a corresponding end tag. For example, for each <dsml:attr> tag, there is a corresponding </dsml:attr> to end the attr entry in the DSML document.

```
<dsml:objectclass>
  <dsml:oc-value>top</dsml:oc-value>
  <dsml:oc-value>person</dsml:oc-value>
  <dsml:oc-value>organizationalPerson</dsml:oc-value>
  <dsml:oc-value>inetOrgPerson</dsml:oc-value>
</dsml:objectclass>
<dsml:attr name="cn">
  <dsml:value>Barney Fife</dsml:value>
</dsml:attr>
<dsml:attr name="sn">
  <dsml:value>Fife</dsml:value>
</dsml:attr>
<dsml:attr name="uid">
  <dsml:value>bfife</dsml:value>
</dsml:attr>
<dsml:attr name="description">
  <dsml:value>Deputy Sheriff</dsml:value>
</dsml:attr>
<dsml:attr name="mail">
  <dsml:value>bfife@dtasi.com</dsml:value>
</dsml:attr>
</dsml:entry>
</dsml:directory-entries>
</dsml:dsml>
```

Figure 11.7   *Example DSML file (continued)*

Figure 11.6 shows that a DSML file that contains Directory entries consists of the standard DSML header tag, followed by the DSML Directory-entries tag, which is in turn followed by one or more DSML entry tags. The standard DSML header tag in the first line of the above file must be included verbatim in every DSML document so that the document can be recognized as such. Figure 11.7 shows a DSML document corresponding to the LDIF file shown in Figure 11.2.

Notice that multivalued attributes are well supported by having a separate entry for each value within the attr entry. For example,

```
<dsml:attr name="cn">
  <dsml:value>Bruce Greenblatt</dsml:value>
  <dsml:value>Bruce G Greenblatt</dsml:value>
</dsml:attr>
```

gives a cn attribute with two values. To a certain extent, DSML is just a more verbose version of LDIF. But, because many other services are making use of XML, and no other services use LDIF, the use of XML for conveying LDAP information in a file format is more attractive. One of the important pieces of work to be done in order for DSML to be successful is its integration with other DTDs. As a standalone format, DSML is bound to be somewhat successful, but once it is integrated into other document types, its success will be much greater. For example, consider the integration of a DSML document into multimedia content. Directory information that is related to the words, pictures, videos, sounds, and so on, in the multimedia content provides for many possibilities for the display of the multimedia document. This is especially true once the DSML consortium has added the capabilities of access control information. By embedding rights and other access control data in the document, different presentations can be made depending upon which user is viewing the document.

Another possibility for a future enhancement to DSML is the ability for the DMSL document to hold Directory operations. One of the nice features of LDIF is this ability. Some LDAP-enabled applications use an LDIF file as part of the install process. Instead of using native LDAP code, as specified in Chapter 9, to enhance the schema and create other required LDAP entries, some applications include an LDIF file that represents the changes that are needed to the schema and the DIT. Then these applications launch a common tool that manipulates the LDIF file to update the Directory. Whenever the install procedure is changed for new initial DIT entries or schema, the install program does not need to be changed. Instead, just the LDIF file is changed. This new feature is expected in DSML 2.0.

This chapter has shown how Directory information can be formatted in XML using the constructs of DSML. This allows for easy interaction with other applications that understand XML, such as Web Browsers. Another key user of XML data is the Metadirectory application. Metadirectories create a consistent view of the many sources of Directory information that exist in the enterprise.

INDEX